The COMIC BOOK BIBLE

Written and Illustrated by
Rob Suggs

Coloring by
Christopher "Scribble Boy" Gray

BARBOUR
PUBLISHING

ISBN 978-1-57748-143-0

All Scripture quotations are from The King James Version of the Bible.

Published by Barbour Publishing, Inc., P.O. Box 719, Uhrichsville, Ohio 44683, www.barbourbooks.com

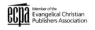 Member of the
Evangelical Christian
Publishers Association

Printed in China.

The COMIC BOOK BOOK BIBLE

TABLE OF CONTENTS

THE OLD TESTAMENT

TABLE OF CONTENTS

THE NEW TESTAMENT

MAPS

THE STORY OF CREATION

IN THE BEGINNING GOD CREATED THE HEAVEN AND THE EARTH. AND THE
EARTH WAS WITHOUT FORM, AND VOID; . . . .
GENESIS 1:1, 2

IN THE BEGINNING, GOD
CREATED EVERYTHING. THE
EARTH WAS EMPTY AND FORMLESS.

DARKNESS WAS EVERYWHERE, AND GOD'S SPIRIT HOVERED OVER THE WATERS.

The Story of Creation ⬤6 Genesis 1 and 2

AND DARKNESS WAS UPON THE FACE OF THE DEEP. AND THE SPIRIT OF GOD MOVED UPON THE FACE OF THE WATERS.
GENESIS 1:2

AND GOD SAID, "LET THERE BE LIGHT!"

HE CALLED THE LIGHT "DAY," AND THE DARKNESS "NIGHT." EVENING AND MORNING: THE FIRST DAY!

ON THE SECOND DAY, HE CREATED THE SKY AND THE CLOUDS.

THEN HE FILLED THE EARTH WITH GRASS, TREES, AND FLOWERS ON THE THIRD DAY.

AND GOD SAID, LET THERE BE LIGHTS IN THE FIRMAMENT
OF THE HEAVEN TO DIVIDE THE DAY FROM THE NIGHT; . . . .
GENESIS 1:14

ON THE FOURTH DAY, HE MADE THE SUN, THE MOON, AND THE STARS
FOR LIGHT — AND TO MARK THE SEASONS.

ON THE FIFTH DAY, HE FILLED THE
WATERS WITH LIVING THINGS, AND
THE SKIES WITH BIRDS.

ON THE SIXTH DAY, HE MADE ALL
THE ANIMALS OF THE EARTH.
BUT ONE THING WAS STILL MISSING.

The Story of Creation ⟨ 8 ⟩ Genesis 1 and 2

AND GOD SAID, LET US MAKE MAN IN OUR IMAGE, AFTER OUR LIKENESS:
AND LET THEM HAVE DOMINION. . .OVER ALL
THE EARTH . . . .   **GENESIS 1:26**

IN HIS OWN LIKENESS, HE CREATED THE FIRST MAN AND THE FIRST WOMAN: ADAM AND EVE.

THEY WERE TO TEND THEIR BEAUTIFUL GARDEN, EDEN, AND TO NAME AND CARE FOR ALL THE ANIMALS.

THEN IT WAS THE SEVENTH DAY — AND GOD RESTED.

The Story of Creation ⑨ **Genesis 1 and 2**

THE STORY OF ADAM AND EVE

AND GOD SAID, BEHOLD, I HAVE GIVEN YOU EVERY HERB BEARING SEED,
... AND EVERY TREE; ... TO YOU IT SHALL BE FOR MEAT.

GENESIS 1:29

GOD HAS GIVEN US EVERYTHING WE COULD EVER NEED!

HE MUST REALLY LOVE US!

STILL — DON'T YOU WONDER ABOUT THIS TREE?

YES. BUT YOU KNOW THAT'S THE ONLY TREE GOD WARNED US ABOUT.

ITS FRUIT IS OFF LIMITS.

HMMM. WE'LL SEE ABOUT THAT!

. . . AND HE [THE SERPENT] SAID UNTO THE WOMAN, YEA, HATH GOD SAID, YE SHALL NOT EAT OF EVERY TREE OF THE GARDEN?   GENESIS 3:1

. . . AND ADAM AND HIS WIFE HID THEMSELVES FROM THE
PRESENCE OF THE LORD GOD AMONGST THE TREES
OF THE GARDEN.   GENESIS 3:8

The Story of Adam and Eve ⟨12⟩ Genesis 3 and 4

...AND THE LORD HAD RESPECT UNTO ABEL AND TO HIS OFFERING: BUT UNTO CAIN AND TO HIS OFFERING HE HAD NOT RESPECT.... GENESIS 4:4-5

THE STORY OF NOAH

AND GOD SAID UNTO NOAH . . . MAKE THEE AN ARK OF GOPHER
WOOD; . . . AND OF EVERY LIVING OF ALL FLESH, TWO OF EVERY SORT
SHALT THOU BRING INTO THE ARK . . . .   GENESIS 6:13, 19

WHAT EVIL TIMES! PEOPLE WORSHIP EVERY KIND OF *IDOL!*

COME ON, NOAH, LIVE A LITTLE. YOUR GOD WON'T CARE!

YES, LORD, I HEAR YOU. WHAT DO YOU WANT ME TO DO?

FAMILY, THE LORD HAS RUN OUT OF PATIENCE. HE WANTS TO CLEANSE THE EARTH AND MAKE A FRESH START, AND WE HAVE A BUILDING PROJECT...

THUS DID NOAH; ACCORDING TO ALL THAT GOD
COMMANDED HIM, SO DID HE.   GENESIS 6:22

THERE WENT IN TWO AND TWO UNTO NOAH INTO THE ARK,
... AND IT CAME TO PASS AFTER SEVEN DAYS, THAT THE WATERS OF THE
FLOOD WERE UPON THE EARTH.   **GENESIS 7:9-10**

HERE COME THE ANIMALS — JUST AS GOD SAID!

SAY, HERE COMES THE RAIN — JUST AS NOAH SAID!

SOON...

THE FLOOD WASHED AWAY OUR HOMES — HOW LONG BEFORE IT COVERS THESE HILLS? I WISH WE WERE ON THE BOAT!

ON THE ARK...

FATHER, THE RAIN STOPPED AFTER 40 DAYS. AND THE FLOOD HAS BEEN RECEDING FOR WEEKS.

YES, SON — THAT'S WHY I'M RELEASING A DOVE. IF IT DOESN'T COME BACK, IT HAS FOUND DRY LAND.

AND GOD SPAKE UNTO NOAH, SAYING, GO FORTH OF THE ARK, THOU,
AND THY WIFE, AND THY SONS, AND THY SONS' WIVES WITH THEE.
GENESIS 8:15-16

THE STORY OF ABRAHAM

NOW THE LORD HAD SAID UNTO ABRAM, GET THEE OUT OF THY COUNTRY,
AND FROM THY KINDRED, AND FROM THY FATHER'S HOUSE, UNTO A LAND
THAT I WILL SHEW THEE.   GENESIS 12:1

GENERATIONS AFTER NOAH,
GOD SPOKE TO A MAN NAMED
ABRAHAM.

ABRAM, LEAVE YOUR COUNTRY,
YOUR PEOPLE, AND YOUR FAMILY,
AND GO TO THE LAND I WILL
SHOW YOU.
YOU WILL BE THE FIRST OF A
GREAT NATION, AND I WILL
BLESS YOU. I WILL MAKE
YOUR NAME GREAT, AND YOU
WILL BE A BLESSING TO OTHERS.
I WILL BLESS THOSE WHO
BLESS YOU, AND I WILL
CURSE THOSE WHO
CURSE YOU!

OH, ABRAHAM,
I KNOW WHAT GOD
SAID — BUT WE'RE
GETTING OLDER, AND
HAVE NO CHILDREN.

IS THIS
HOW GOD REWARDS
YOUR LIFE OF
OBEDIENCE?

SARAI,
GOD HAS SPOKEN,
AND ALL WE CAN DO
IS WAIT AND
TRUST.

AND HE SAID, I WILL CERTAINLY RETURN UNTO THEE ACCORDING TO THE TIME OF LIFE, AND, LO, SARAH THY WIFE SHALL HAVE A SON. AND SARAH HEARD IT IN THE TENT DOOR, WHICH WAS BEHIND HIM.

GENESIS 18:10

AND ABRAHAM WAS AN HUNDRED YEARS OLD, WHEN HIS SON ISAAC
WAS BORN UNTO HIM. AND SARAH SAID, GOD HATH MADE ME TO LAUGH,
SO THAT ALL THAT HEAR WILL LAUGH WITH ME.   **GENESIS 21: 5, 6**

. . . AND ABRAHAM BUILT AN ALTAR THERE, AND LAID THE WOOD IN ORDER, AND BOUND ISAAC HIS SON, AND LAID HIM ON THE ALTAR UPON THE WOOD.　　GENESIS 22:9

THE STORY OF JACOB AND ESAU

... THE ONE PEOPLE SHALL BE STRONGER THAN THE OTHER PEOPLE; AND THE ELDER SHALL SERVE THE YOUNGER.   GENESIS 25:23

ISAAC AND REBEKAH HAD TWO SONS. ESAU WAS THE FIRSTBORN BY A FEW SECONDS, BUT JACOB CAME INTO THE WORLD GRIPPING HIS ANKLE; THEIR TWO LIVES CONTINUED THIS THEME.

JACOB LIVES UP TO HIS NAME — "THE DECEIVER." HE'S ALWAYS FOOLING HIS BROTHER.

WELL — GO EASY ON HIM — YOU KNOW HE'S MY FAVORITE.

YOU LIKE ESAU BEST BECAUSE HE HUNTS AND STAYS IN THE FIELDS!

IT'S NOT FAIR THAT ESAU SHOULD RULE THE TRIBE JUST BECAUSE HE'S A FEW SECONDS OLDER. I'M SMARTER AND I'LL PROVE IT —

BY GETTING THAT BIRTHRIGHT FROM HIM!

AND JACOB SOD [COOKED] POTTAGE: AND ESAU CAME
FROM THE FIELD, AND HE WAS FAINT.
GENESIS 25:29

AND JACOB SAID UNTO HIS FATHER, I AM ESAU THY FIRSTBORN; I HAVE
DONE ACCORDING AS THOU BADEST ME: ARISE, I PRAY THEE, SIT AND
EAT OF MY VENISON, THAT THY SOUL MAY BLESS ME.   **GENESIS 27:19**

The Story of Jacob and Esau （24） **Genesis 27 through 33**

AND HE DREAMED, AND BEHOLD A LADDER SET UP ON THE EARTH, AND THE TOP OF IT REACHED TO HEAVEN: AND BEHOLD THE ANGELS OF GOD ASCENDING AND DESCENDING ON IT. **GENESIS 28:12**

SLEEPING UNDER THE STARS, JACOB HAS AN INCREDIBLE DREAM.

I AM THE LORD YOUR GOD, GOD OF ABRAHAM AND ISAAC. I WILL BE WITH YOU, AND YOUR CHILDREN WILL SPREAD OUT ACROSS THE EARTH. I WILL NEVER LEAVE YOU, JACOB.

SURELY THE LORD IS IN THIS PLACE AND I DIDN'T REALIZE IT!

YEARS LATER, ESAU RECEIVES A MESSAGE.

JACOB WANTS HIS MASTER ESAU TO KNOW HE HAS GROWN WEALTHY, AND HE SENDS THIS MESSAGE TO SEEK YOUR FAVOR AND FORGIVENESS.

ESAU IS COMING TO MEET YOU WITH 400 MEN.

I MUST SEND MY FAMILY AWAY. THEY MAY BE COMING TO KILL ME!

BUT...

JACOB, I'VE MISSED YOU!

ESAU, GOD HAS CHANGED ME. LET'S PUT THE PAST BEHIND US!

THE STORY OF JOSEPH

NOW ISRAEL [JACOB] LOVED JOSEPH MORE THAN ALL HIS CHILDREN,
BECAUSE HE WAS THE SON OF HIS OLD AGE: AND HE MADE HIM A COAT
OF MANY COLOURS.   GENESIS 37:3

AND HIS BRETHREN SAID TO HIM, SHALT THOU INDEED REIGN OVER US? OR SHALT THOU INDEED HAVE DOMINION OVER US? AND THEY HATED HIM YET THE MORE FOR HIS DREAMS, AND FOR HIS WORDS.   GENESIS 37:8

COME, AND LET US SELL HIM TO THE ISHMEELITES, AND LET NOT OUR HAND BE UPON HIM; FOR HE IS OUR BROTHER AND OUR FLESH. AND HIS BRETHREN WERE CONTENT. **GENESIS 37:27**

The Story of Joseph (28) **Genesis 37 through 39**

AND JOSEPH'S MASTER TOOK HIM, AND PUT HIM INTO THE PRISON, A PLACE WHERE THE KING'S PRISONERS WERE BOUND: AND HE WAS THERE IN THE PRISON.   GENESIS 39:20

JOSEPH IN EGYPT

... WE HAVE DREAMED A DREAM, AND THERE IS NO INTERPRETER OF IT.
AND JOSEPH SAID UNTO THEM, DO NOT INTERPRETATIONS BELONG TO
GOD? TELL ME THEM, I PRAY YOU.

GENESIS 40:8

AND JOSEPH WAS THE GOVERNOR OVER THE LAND . . . AND JOSEPH'S BRETHREN CAME, AND BOWED DOWN THEMSELVES BEFORE HIM WITH THEIR FACES TO THE EARTH.   GENESIS 42:6

THEN JOSEPH COMMANDED TO FILL THEIR SACKS WITH CORN, AND TO RESTORE EVERY MAN'S MONEY INTO HIS SACK, AND TO GIVE THEM PROVISION FOR THE WAY . . . .   GENESIS 42:25

AND JOSEPH SAID UNTO HIS BRETHREN, COME NEAR TO ME, I PRAY YOU.
AND THEY CAME NEAR. AND HE SAID, I AM JOSEPH YOUR BROTHER,
WHOM YE SOLD INTO EGYPT.   GENESIS 45:4

THE STORY OF MOSES

AND WHEN SHE COULD NOT LONGER HIDE HIM, SHE TOOK FOR HIM AN ARK OF BULRUSHES, AND DAUBED IT WITH SLIME AND WITH PITCH, AND PUT THE CHILD THEREIN; AND SHE LAID IT IN THE FLAGS BY THE RIVER'S BRINK.   EXODUS 2:3

STILL TOO MANY JEWS! I'LL HAVE ALL THEIR BABIES THROWN INTO THE RIVER!

JACOB'S SONS HAD CHILDREN, AND GRANDCHILDREN. YEARS LATER THERE WERE THOUSANDS OF HEBREWS IN EGYPT — BUT THEY BECAME SLAVES.

ONE FAMILY PLOTS TO SAVE THEIR BABY SON.

MY BASKET IS FINISHED. COME WITH ME TO THE RIVER, MIRIAM.

HE'LL BE SAFE FROM PHARAOH HERE. MIRIAM, YOU'LL STAY HIDDEN AND WATCH.

THE EGYPTIAN PRINCESS SEES THE BABY.

LOOK! A BABY IN A BASKET.

GIRL, DO YOU KNOW OF A HEBREW NURSE TO HELP CARE FOR THIS CHILD?

YES! MY MOTHER CAN DO IT!

SO THE HEBREW BOY WAS CARED FOR BY HIS OWN FAMILY — AND RAISED IN PHARAOH'S FAMILY.

AND HE LOOKED THIS WAY AND THAT WAY, AND WHEN HE SAW THAT
THERE WAS NO MAN, HE SLEW THE EGYPTIAN, AND HID HIM IN THE SAND.
EXODUS 2:12

COME NOW THEREFORE, AND I WILL SEND THEE UNTO PHARAOH,
THAT THOU MAYEST BRING FORTH MY PEOPLE THE CHILDREN OF ISRAEL
OUT OF EGYPT.   EXODUS 3:10

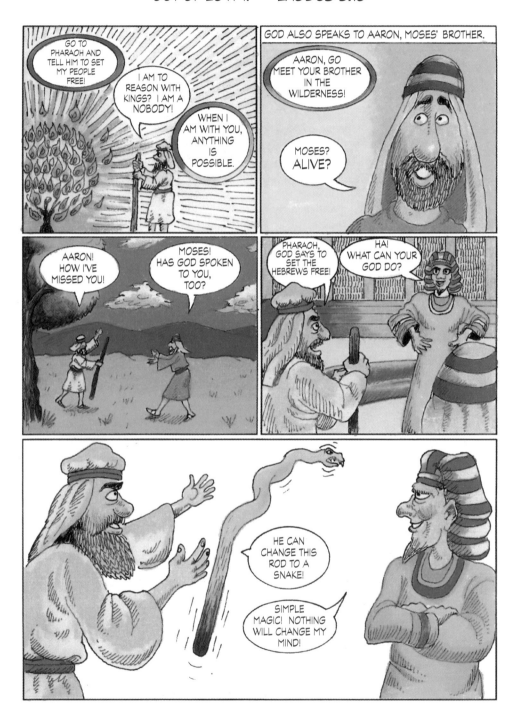

The Story of Moses (36) Exodus 1 through 12

AND I WILL STRETCH OUT MY HAND, AND SMITE EGYPT WITH
ALL MY WONDERS WHICH I WILL DO IN THE MIDST THEREOF:
AND AFTER THAT HE WILL LET YOU GO.   EXODUS 3:20

MOSES AND THE EXODUS

AND THE CHILDREN OF ISRAEL JOURNEYED ... ABOUT SIX HUNDRED THOUSAND ON FOOT THAT WERE MEN, BESIDE CHILDREN ... AND FLOCKS, AND HERDS, EVEN VERY MUCH CATTLE.   EXODUS 12:37-38

BUT LIFT THOU UP THY ROD, AND STRETCH OUT THINE HAND OVER THE SEA, AND DIVIDE IT: AND THE CHILDREN OF ISRAEL SHALL GO ON DRY GROUND THROUGH THE MIDST OF THE SEA.   EXODUS 14:16

AND THE LORD CAME DOWN UPON MOUNT SINAI, ON THE TOP OF THE MOUNT: AND THE LORD CALLED MOSES UP TO THE TOP OF THE MOUNT; AND MOSES WENT UP.   EXODUS 19:20

AND LET THEM MAKE ME A SANCTUARY; THAT I MAY DWELL AMONG
THEM. ACCORDING TO ALL THAT I SHEW THEE, AFTER THE PATTERN OF
THE TABERNACLE, AND THE PATTERN OF ALL THE INSTRUMENTS THEREOF,
EVEN SO SHALL YE MAKE IT.   EXODUS 25:8-9

"WE ARE TO BUILD A HOUSE OF GOD — A TABERNACLE. IT WILL BE A PLACE FOR THE
SACRED ARK HOLDING THE TABLETS I BROUGHT DOWN FROM SINAI."

FROM THEN ON, THE ARK IS CARRIED IN FRONT. THEY FOLLOW GOD'S CLOUD TO THE PROMISED LAND.

JOSHUA AND CALEB

FOR I KNOW THY REBELLION, AND THY STIFF NECK: BEHOLD, WHILE I AM
YET ALIVE WITH YOU THIS DAY, YE HAVE BEEN REBELLIOUS AGAINST
THE LORD . . . . DEUTERONOMY 31:27

SEND THOU MEN, THAT THEY MAY SEARCH THE LAND OF CANAAN, WHICH I GIVE UNTO THE CHILDREN OF ISRAEL: OF EVERY TRIBE OF THEIR FATHERS SHALL YE SEND A MAN . . . . NUMBERS 13:2

AND THERE WE SAW THE GIANTS, THE SONS OF ANAK, WHICH COME OF THE GIANTS: AND WE WERE IN OUR OWN SIGHT AS GRASSHOPPERS, AND SO WE WERE IN THEIR SIGHT. NUMBERS 13:33

SURELY THEY SHALL NOT SEE THE LAND WHICH I SWARE UNTO THEIR FATHERS, NEITHER SHALL ANY OF THEM THAT PROVOKED ME SEE IT.
NUMBERS 14:23

JOSHUA AT JERICHO

AND JOSHUA THE SON OF NUN SENT OUT OF SHITTIM TWO MEN TO SPY
SECRETLY, SAYING, GO VIEW THE LAND, EVEN JERICHO . . . .
JOSHUA 2:1

BEHOLD, WHEN WE COME INTO THE LAND, THOU SHALT BIND THIS LINE OF SCARLET THREAD IN THE WINDOW WHICH THOU DIDST LET US DOWN BY .... JOSHUA 2:18

AND THE PRIESTS THAT BARE THE ARK OF THE COVENANT OF THE LORD STOOD FIRM ON DRY GROUND IN THE MIDST OF JORDAN, AND ALL THE ISRAELITES PASSED OVER ON DRY GROUND . . . .   JOSHUA 3:17

SO THE ISRAELITES CROSS THE JORDAN, AND AS THE ARK REACHES THE RIVER, THE WATERS STOP FLOWING — JUST AS IN MOSES' TIME!

JOSHUA MEETS A STRANGER.

WHO ARE YOU?

CAPTAIN OF GOD'S ARMY. TAKE OFF YOUR SHOES. YOU ARE ON HOLY GROUND.

HERE ARE YOUR ORDERS.

THE ISRAELITES PLACE 7 PRIESTS WITH TRUMPETS AT THE HEAD OF THE LINE.

AND YE SHALL COMPASS THE CITY, ALL YE MEN OF WAR, AND GO
ROUND ABOUT THE CITY ONCE. THUS SHALT THOU DO SIX DAYS.
JOSHUA 6:3

DEBORAH THE JUDGE

AND THE LORD SOLD THEM INTO THE HAND OF JABIN KING OF CANAAN,
THAT REIGNED IN HAZOR; THE CAPTAIN OF WHOSE HOST
WAS SISERA . . . .   JUDGES 4:2

WE WORSHIP THE SUN GOD!

BLESS OUR LABOR AND OUR CROPS!

AFTER THE TIME OF MOSES AND JOSHUA, THE ISRAELITES SETTLED IN CANAAN. THEY NO
LONGER NEEDED GOD'S CLOUD TO GUIDE THEM THROUGH THE DESERT, OR HIS MANNA FOR
FOOD, AND THEY BEGAN TO FORGET THE TRUE GOD.

THE MORE THEY FORGOT GOD, THE WEAKER THEY BECAME — AND OTHER TRIBES RAIDED THEM.

IT'S KING JABIN'S MEN — STEALING OUR GRAIN!

THE ISRAELITES DEPENDED ON LEADERS CALLED JUDGES.

DEBORAH WILL KNOW WHAT TO DO.

HELP US, DEBORAH! IT'S KING JABIN AGAIN RAIDING OUR HOMES!

AND SHE DWELT UNDER THE PALM TREE OF DEBORAH BETWEEN RAMAH AND BETH-EL IN MOUNT EPHRAIM: AND THE CHILDREN OF ISRAEL CAME UP TO HER FOR JUDGMENT.   JUDGES 4:5

AND DEBORAH SAID UNTO BARAK, UP; FOR THIS IS THE DAY IN WHICH THE LORD HATH DELIVERED SISERA INTO THINE HAND: IS NOT THE LORD GONE OUT BEFORE THEE? . . . .   **JUDGES 4:14**

... AND ALL THE HOST OF SISERA FELL UPON THE EDGE OF THE SWORD; AND THERE WAS NOT A MAN LEFT. HOWBEIT SISERA FLED AWAY ON HIS FEET TO THE TENT .... **JUDGES 4:16-17**

THE STORY OF GIDEON

. . . AND HIS SON GIDEON THRESHED WHEAT BY THE WINEPRESS, TO HIDE IT FROM THE MIDIANITES. AND THE ANGEL OF THE LORD APPEARED UNTO HIM, AND SAID UNTO HIM, THE LORD IS WITH THEE, THOU MIGHTY MAN OF VALOUR.   JUDGES 6:11-12

AND GIDEON SAID UNTO GOD, IF THOU WILT SAVE ISRAEL BY MINE HAND,
AS THOU HAST SAID, BEHOLD, I WILL PUT A FLEECE OF WOOL
IN THE FLOOR . . . .   JUDGES 6:36-37

NOW THEREFORE GO TO, PROCLAIM IN THE EARS OF THE PEOPLE, SAYING, WHOSOEVER IS FEARFUL AND AFRAID, LET HIM RETURN AND DEPART EARLY FROM MOUNT GILEAD.   JUDGES 7:3

... BEHOLD, I DREAMED A DREAM, AND, LO, A CAKE OF BARLEY BREAD TUMBLED INTO THE HOST OF MIDIAN, AND CAME UNTO A TENT, AND SMOTE IT THAT IT FELL, AND OVERTURNED IT, THAT THE TENT LAY ALONG.

JUDGES 7:13

The Story of Gideon (57) Judges 6 and 7

THE STORY OF SAMSON

AND THE WOMAN BARE A SON, AND CALLED HIS NAME SAMSON: AND
THE CHILD GREW, AND THE LORD BLESSED HIM.
JUDGES 13:24

THE PHILISTINES BECOME THE GREATEST ENEMY TO GOD'S PEOPLE. BUT AN ANGEL APPEARS TO A CHILDLESS COUPLE.

YOU WILL HAVE A CHILD, AND HE WILL HELP DEFEAT THE PHILISTINES; BUT NEVER CUT HIS HAIR.

AS SAMSON GROWS, SO DOES HIS STRENGTH.

NO ONE ELSE CAN STOP A LION. BUT I'D RATHER STOP THE PHILISTINES!

WAS THIS DOOR SUPPOSED TO HOLD ME? SEND ME THE BILL.

THE PHILISTINES TRAP HIM IN THE CITY ONE NIGHT.

WE'VE LOCKED THE GATES. SOON WE'LL JUMP HIM.

AND DELILAH SAID TO SAMSON, TELL ME, I PRAY THEE, WHEREIN THY GREAT STRENGTH LIETH, AND WHEREWITH THOU MIGHTEST BE BOUND TO AFFLICT THEE.　**JUDGES 16:6**

...IF I BE SHAVEN, THEN MY STRENGTH WILL GO FROM ME, AND I SHALL BECOME WEAK, AND BE LIKE ANY OTHER MAN.

JUDGES 16:17

... O LORD GOD, REMEMBER ME, I PRAY THEE, AND STRENGTHEN ME, I PRAY THEE, ONLY THIS ONCE, O GOD, THAT I MAY BE AT ONCE AVENGED OF THE PHILISTINES FOR MY TWO EYES.   JUDGES 16:28

THE STORY OF RUTH

... FOR WHITHER THOU GOEST, I WILL GO; AND WHERE THOU LODGEST, I WILL LODGE: THY PEOPLE SHALL BE MY PEOPLE, AND THY GOD MY GOD.

RUTH 1:16

THEN SAID BOAZ UNTO RUTH, HEAREST THOU NOT, MY DAUGHTER? GO NOT TO GLEAN IN ANOTHER FIELD, NEITHER GO FROM HENCE, BUT ABIDE HERE FAST BY MY MAIDENS.   RUTH 2:8

AND NOW, MY DAUGHTER, FEAR NOT; I WILL DO TO THEE ALL THAT THOU REQUIREST: FOR ALL THE CITY OF MY PEOPLE DOTH KNOW THAT THOU ART A VIRTUOUS WOMAN.　　**RUTH 3:11**

AND THE WOMEN HER NEIGHBOURS GAVE IT A NAME, SAYING, THERE IS A SON BORN TO NAOMI; AND THEY CALLED HIS NAME OBED: HE IS THE FATHER OF JESSE, THE FATHER OF DAVID.   RUTH 4:17

THE STORY OF SAMUEL

AND SHE VOWED A VOW, AND SAID, O LORD OF HOSTS, IF THOU WILT
... GIVE UNTO THINE HANDMAID A MAN CHILD, THEN I WILL GIVE HIM
UNTO THE LORD ALL THE DAYS OF HIS LIFE ....   1 SAMUEL 1:11

THEREFORE ALSO I HAVE LENT HIM TO THE LORD; AS LONG AS HE LIVETH HE SHALL BE LENT TO THE LORD. AND HE WORSHIPPED THE LORD THERE.   1 SAMUEL 1:28

AND THE LORD CALLED YET AGAIN, SAMUEL. AND SAMUEL AROSE AND WENT TO ELI, AND SAID, HERE AM I; FOR THOU DIDST CALL ME. AND HE ANSWERED, I CALLED NOT, MY SON . . . .   1 SAMUEL 3:6

AND THE LORD SAID TO SAMUEL, BEHOLD, I WILL DO A THING IN ISRAEL, AT WHICH BOTH THE EARS OF EVERY ONE THAT HEARETH IT SHALL TINGLE.   1 SAMUEL 3:11

ISRAEL'S FIRST KING

AND [THE ELDERS OF ISRAEL] SAID UNTO HIM, BEHOLD, THOU ART OLD, AND THY SONS WALK NOT IN THY WAYS: NOW MAKE US A KING TO JUDGE US LIKE ALL THE NATIONS.   1 SAMUEL 8:5

FOR MANY YEARS, SAMUEL SERVES AS JUDGE, LEADING THE ISRAELITES TO MANY VICTORIES AND KEEPING THEM FAITHFUL TO GOD.

IN MEMORY OF TODAY'S VICTORY WE LIFT UP THIS STONE AND NAME IT "EBENEZER."

IT MEANS "GOD HAS LED US THUS FAR."

SAMUEL, YOU'VE BEEN A GREAT LEADER — BUT YOU'RE GETTING OLD.

MY SONS CAN REPLACE ME.

NO, SAMUEL, WE WANT A KING — LIKE OTHER NATIONS! APPOINT ONE FOR US.

BUT YOU DON'T NEED A KING BETWEEN YOU AND GOD. HE WILL GUIDE YOU MORE WISELY THAN ANY KING.

AND WHEN SAMUEL SAW SAUL, THE LORD SAID UNTO HIM, BEHOLD THE MAN WHOM I SPAKE TO THEE OF! THIS SAME SHALL REIGN OVER MY PEOPLE.   1 SAMUEL 9:17

THEREFORE THEY ENQUIRED OF THE LORD FURTHER, IF THE MAN SHOULD YET COME THITHER. AND THE LORD ANSWERED, BEHOLD, HE HATH HID HIMSELF AMONG THE STUFF.   1 SAMUEL 10:22

AND SAMUEL SAID TO SAUL, THOU HAST DONE FOOLISHLY: THOU HAST NOT KEPT THE COMMANDMENT OF THE LORD THY GOD, WHICH HE COMMANDED THEE . . . .   1 SAMUEL 13:13

SAUL FINALLY ACCEPTS HIS DESTINY AND GOES INTO BATTLE.

THE LORD HAS BEEN WITH US! SAUL IS A PRETTY GOOD KING IF YOU ASK ME.

I LIKE BEING KING BETTER THAN I EXPECTED — IT'S OBVIOUS I HAVE NATURAL TALENT!

WAIT 'TIL I SHOW THEM IN THIS NEXT BIG BATTLE!

KING, WE CAN'T FIGHT 'TIL WE'VE MADE AN OFFERING TO GOD — BUT SAMUEL IS MISSING, AND TIME IS RUNNING OUT!

WELL, FORGET SAMUEL — I'LL MAKE THE SACRIFICE! WE'RE HERE TO *FIGHT*, NOT SIT AROUND WAITING FOR OLD PROPHETS!

SAUL, YOU DISOBEYED GOD WHEN YOU MADE THE OFFERING YOURSELF; HE IS ANGRY!

DON'T SPEAK TO YOUR KING LIKE THAT.

FROM THIS TIME ON, SAUL BEGINS TO LOSE GOD'S POWER — AND A NEW PHILISTINE THREAT APPEARS!

IT'S THE GIANT GOLIATH! NO ISRAELITE WILL DARE TO FACE HIM!

DAVID AND GOLIATH

THEN SAMUEL TOOK THE HORN OF OIL, AND ANOINTED HIM IN THE MIDST OF HIS BRETHREN: AND THE SPIRIT OF THE LORD CAME UPON DAVID FROM THAT DAY FORWARD . . . . 1 SAMUEL 16:13

AND DAVID ROSE UP EARLY IN THE MORNING, AND LEFT THE SHEEP WITH A KEEPER, . . . AND HE CAME TO THE TRENCH, AS THE HOST WAS GOING FORTH TO THE FIGHT, AND SHOUTED FOR THE BATTLE.

1 SAMUEL 17:20

AND DAVID PUT HIS HAND IN HIS BAG, AND TOOK THENCE A STONE, AND
SLANG IT, AND SMOTE THE PHILISTINE IN HIS FOREHEAD; AND HE FELL
UPON HIS FACE TO THE EARTH.

1 SAMUEL 17:49

David and Goliath   77   1 Samuel 16 and 17

DAVID THE KING

AND DAVID PERCEIVED THAT THE LORD HAD ESTABLISHED HIM KING OVER ISRAEL, AND THAT HE HAD EXALTED HIS KINGDOM FOR HIS PEOPLE ISRAEL'S SAKE.   **2 SAMUEL 5:12**

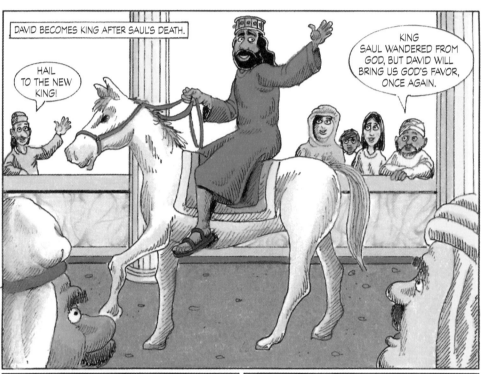

DAVID BECOMES KING AFTER SAUL'S DEATH.

HAIL TO THE NEW KING!

KING SAUL WANDERED FROM GOD, BUT DAVID WILL BRING US GOD'S FAVOR, ONCE AGAIN.

UNDER HIS LEADERSHIP, ISRAEL IS POWERFUL.

WE USED TO HUMILIATE THE ISRAELITES. NOW THE TABLES ARE TURNED.

NATHAN, YOU ARE GOD'S PROPHET. DON'T YOU THINK WE SHOULD HONOR GOD IN JERUSALEM BY BRINGING BACK THE ARK OF THE COVENANT?

YES! PUT IT WHERE THE PEOPLE CAN SEE IT!

AND DAVID AROSE, AND WENT WITH ALL THE PEOPLE THAT WERE WITH HIM FROM BAALE OF JUDAH, TO BRING UP FROM THENCE THE ARK OF GOD . . . .   2 SAMUEL 6:2

THE ARK HOLDING THE 10 COMMANDMENTS HAD BEEN NEARLY FORGOTTEN. NOW, DAVID BRINGS IT INTO JERUSALEM WITH MUSIC AND CELEBRATION!

LORD, THE HOLY ARK IS DISPLAYED IN A TATTERED TENT. I WOULD LIKE TO BUILD A HOUSE THAT IS WORTHY FOR YOU TO DWELL IN.

NATHAN, GOD HAS SPOKEN TO ME. THE TEMPLE WILL BE BUILT — BUT BY ONE TO COME AFTER ME.

GOD HAS HIS OWN TIMES AND SEASONS.

ALONG WITH THE TRADITION OF THE TIME, DAVID TAKES MANY WIVES.

... AND FROM THE ROOF HE SAW A WOMAN WASHING HERSELF; AND THE WOMAN WAS VERY BEAUTIFUL TO LOOK UPON. AND DAVID SENT AND INQUIRED AFTER THE WOMAN .... 2 SAMUEL 11:2-3

AND DAVID SAID UNTO NATHAN, I HAVE SINNED AGAINST THE LORD. AND NATHAN SAID UNTO DAVID, THE LORD ALSO HATH PUT AWAY THY SIN; THOU SHALT NOT DIE.   2 SAMUEL 12:13

A ROYAL WEDDING.

NATHAN? WHAT DID YOU WANT TO TALK ABOUT?

I'M HERE TO TELL YOU A STORY.

A CERTAIN MAN IN YOUR KINGDOM HAS MORE SHEEP THAN ANYONE. BUT HE SAW ANOTHER MAN WITH ONLY ONE LITTLE LAMB. HE HAD THAT MAN *KILLED* AND TOOK THE LAMB.

THIS IS AN OUTRAGE! WE'LL HAVE THAT MAN *KILLED!*

BUT, SIR...

YOU ARE THE MAN!

DAVID REALIZES HE HAS DONE A TERRIBLE THING. GOD REALIZES IT, TOO. THE FIRST CHILD OF DAVID AND BATHSHEBA DIES. DAVID REPENTS WITH ALL HIS HEART AND SEEKS GOD'S FORGIVENESS.

DAVID AND ABSALOM

. . . AND WHEN I SAY UNTO YOU, SMITE AMNON; THEN KILL HIM, FEAR NOT:
HAVE NOT I COMMANDED YOU? BE COURAGEOUS, AND BE VALIANT.
2 SAMUEL 13:28

DAVID WORKS TO MAKE ISRAEL ONE OF THE WORLD'S GREAT
NATIONS, BUT THERE ARE PROBLEMS IN HIS FAMILY.

ABSALOM, I KNOW AMNON DID SOMETHING TERRIBLE — A WICKED THING. BUT YOU MUST FORGIVE HIM. YOU ARE BOTH MY SONS.

OF COURSE, FATHER. I'M HAVING A FEAST AND AMNON IS INVITED.

AMNON IS INVITED ALL RIGHT — AND WHEN I GIVE THE SIGNAL, YOUR MEN WILL KILL HIM!

WHAT IS GOING ON?

AMNON HURT AND HUMILIATED ABSALOM'S SISTER — HIS OWN HALF-SISTER. ABSALOM SWORE REVENGE.

SO ABSALOM FLED, AND WENT TO GESHUR, AND WAS THERE THREE YEARS. AND THE SOUL OF KING DAVID LONGED TO GO FORTH UNTO ABSALOM . . . . 2 SAMUEL 13:38-39

. . . AND WHEN HE HAD CALLED FOR ABSALOM, HE CAME TO THE KING, AND BOWED HIMSELF ON HIS FACE TO THE GROUND BEFORE THE KING: AND THE KING KISSED ABSALOM.   2 SAMUEL 14:33

. . . AND HIS HEAD CAUGHT HOLD OF THE OAK, AND HE WAS TAKEN UP BETWEEN THE HEAVEN AND THE EARTH; AND THE MULE THAT WAS UNDER HIM WENT AWAY.   2 SAMUEL 18:9

MEN, I BELIEVE THE TIME IS RIGHT. WE HAVE ENOUGH SOLDIERS TO TAKE THE KINGDOM. INVITE ALL THE TRIBES TO HEBRON. WE'LL UNITE THERE AND OVERTHROW MY FATHER!

KING DAVID! YOUR SON IS GATHERING TROOPS AT HEBRON — YOUR LIFE IS IN DANGER!

MY OWN SON! YES, I EXPECTED IT.

I MUST PROTECT MY FAMILY AND LOYAL FRIENDS. WE'LL LEAVE JERUSALEM!

THE BATTLE COMES TO THE FOREST OF EPHRAIM. DAVID'S ARMY OVERWHELMS ABSALOM'S.

AS HE FLEES IN PANIC, ABSALOM'S HAIR IS CAUGHT IN A LOW BRANCH. JOAB'S SOLDIERS KILL HIM THERE.

AGAIN, MY HEART IS BROKEN. I CAN LEAD A NATION, BUT NOT MY OWN FAMILY.

YET THE BEST DAYS ARE STILL TO COME FOR ISRAEL, AND ANOTHER SON OF DAVID.

ISRAEL'S WISEST KING

THEN SAT SOLOMON UPON THE THRONE OF DAVID HIS FATHER; AND HIS KINGDOM WAS ESTABLISHED GREATLY.   1 KINGS 2:12

... AND HE CAME TO JERUSALEM, AND STOOD BEFORE THE ARK OF THE COVENANT OF THE LORD, AND OFFERED UP BURNT-OFFERINGS, AND OFFERED PEACE-OFFERINGS, AND MADE A FEAST TO ALL HIS SERVANTS.

1 KINGS 3:15

Israel's Wisest King (87) 1 Kings 2 and 3

THEN CAME THERE TWO WOMEN, THAT WERE HARLOTS, UNTO THE KING, AND STOOD BEFORE HIM.   1 KINGS 3:16

AND ALL ISRAEL HEARD OF THE JUDGMENT WHICH THE KING HAD JUDGED; AND THEY FEARED THE KING: FOR THEY SAW THAT THE WISDOM OF GOD WAS IN HIM, TO DO JUDGMENT.   1 KINGS 3:28

SOLOMON'S TEMPLE

AND, BEHOLD, I PURPOSE TO BUILD AN HOUSE UNTO THE NAME OF THE
LORD MY GOD, AS THE LORD SPAKE UNTO DAVID MY FATHER . . . .

1 KINGS 5:5

AND HE BUILT THE WALLS OF THE HOUSE WITHIN WITH BOARDS OF
CEDAR, BOTH THE FLOOR OF THE HOUSE, AND THE WALLS OF THE
CEILING: AND HE COVERED THEM ON THE INSIDE WITH WOOD . . . .

1 KINGS 6:15

AND IN THE ELEVENTH YEAR, . . .WAS THE HOUSE FINISHED THROUGH-
OUT ALL THE PARTS THEREOF, AND ACCORDING TO ALL THE FASHION OF
IT. SO WAS HE SEVEN YEARS' IN BUILDING IT.
1 KINGS 6:38

AND AHIJAH CAUGHT THE NEW GARMENT THAT WAS ON HIM, AND RENT IT IN TWELVE PIECES: . . . FOR THUS SAITH THE LORD, THE GOD OF ISRAEL, BEHOLD, I WILL REND THE KINGDOM OUT OF THE HAND OF SOLOMON, AND WILL GIVE TEN TRIBES TO THEE.   1 KINGS 11:30-31

FIRE ON THE MOUNTAIN

SO THEY DIVIDED THE LAND BETWEEN THEM TO PASS THROUGHOUT IT: AHAB WENT ONE WAY BY HIMSELF, AND OBADIAH WENT ANOTHER WAY BY HIMSELF.   1 KINGS 18:6

SOLOMON HAS ALLOWED THE PEOPLE TO WORSHIP FALSE GODS, AND THE LORD IS *NOT* PLEASED.

YOU HAVE DISOBEYED ME, SO YOUR KINGDOM SHALL FALL. BUT BECAUSE OF MY LOVE FOR DAVID, YOUR FATHER, IT WILL NOT HAPPEN DURING YOUR LIFETIME.

THE SPLIT COMES AFTER SOLOMON DIES. THE NORTHERN TRIBES ARE STILL CALLED ISRAEL, WHILE THE SOUTHERN TRIBES ARE CALLED JUDAH.

GREAT SEA

ISRAEL

JUDAH

SALT SEA

ISRAEL'S KING AHAB MARRIES A PRINCESS FROM TYRE, WHERE FALSE GODS WERE WORSHIPED.

MEET JEZEBEL, YOUR QUEEN. YOU WILL OBEY HER AS YOU DO ME!

SO AHAB SENT UNTO ALL THE CHILDREN OF ISRAEL, AND GATHERED THE PROPHETS TOGETHER UNTO MOUNT CARMEL. 1 KINGS 18:20

Fire on the Mountain 96 1 Kings 18

HEAR ME, O LORD, HEAR ME, THAT THIS PEOPLE MAY KNOW THAT THOU ART THE LORD GOD, AND THAT THOU HAST TURNED THEIR HEART BACK AGAIN.   1 KINGS 18:37

A CHARIOT OF FIRE

AND WHEN HE SAW THAT, HE AROSE, AND WENT FOR HIS LIFE, AND CAME TO BEER-SHEBA, WHICH BELONGETH TO JUDAH, AND LEFT HIS SERVANT THERE. BUT HE HIMSELF WENT A DAY'S JOURNEY INTO THE WILDERNESS . . . .   1 KINGS 19:3-4

...FOR THE CHILDREN OF ISRAEL HAVE FORSAKEN THY COVENANT, THROWN DOWN THINE ALTARS, AND SLAIN THY PROPHETS WITH THE SWORD; AND I, EVEN I ONLY, AM LEFT . . . .   1 KINGS 19:10

AND ELIJAH TOOK HIS MANTLE, AND WRAPPED IT TOGETHER, AND SMOTE THE WATERS, AND THEY WERE DIVIDED HITHER AND THITHER, SO THAT THEY TWO WENT OVER ON DRY GROUND.   2 KINGS 2:8

IN ISRAEL AGAIN, ELIJAH FINDS A YOUNG FARMER NAMED ELISHA.

I GIVE YOU MY CLOAK.

THIS MEANS GOD IS CALLING YOU TO BE A PROPHET, TOO.

THIS IS AN HONOR.

FOR YEARS, ELIJAH AND ELISHA TRAVEL TOGETHER.

ELIJAH TEACHES HIS DISCIPLE EVERYTHING HE HAS LEARNED.

ONE DAY, THE TWO SET OUT ON ELIJAH'S FINAL JOURNEY.

SO HOW DO WE CROSS THE JORDAN, ELIJAH?

ELIJAH STRIKES THE WATER WITH HIS CLOAK.

THE RIVER PARTS!

AFTER CROSSING, ELIJAH SAYS GOODBYE.

A Chariot of Fire (100) 1 Kings 19 and 2 Kings 2

. . . . BEHOLD, THERE APPEARED A CHARIOT OF FIRE, AND HORSES OF FIRE, AND PARTED THEM BOTH ASUNDER; AND ELIJAH WENT UP BY A WHIRLWIND INTO HEAVEN.   2 KINGS 2:11

IN A MIGHTY WHIRLWIND, A CHARIOT OF FIRE TAKES ELIJAH INTO THE HEAVENS.

ELIJAH IS ON HIS WAY HOME.

ELISHA THE PROPHET

NOW THERE CRIED A CERTAIN WOMAN OF THE WIVES OF THE SONS OF THE PROPHETS UNTO ELISHA, SAYING, THY SERVANT MY HUSBAND IS DEAD ... AND THE CREDITOR IS COME TO TAKE UNTO HIM MY TWO SONS TO BE BONDMEN.   2 KINGS 4:1

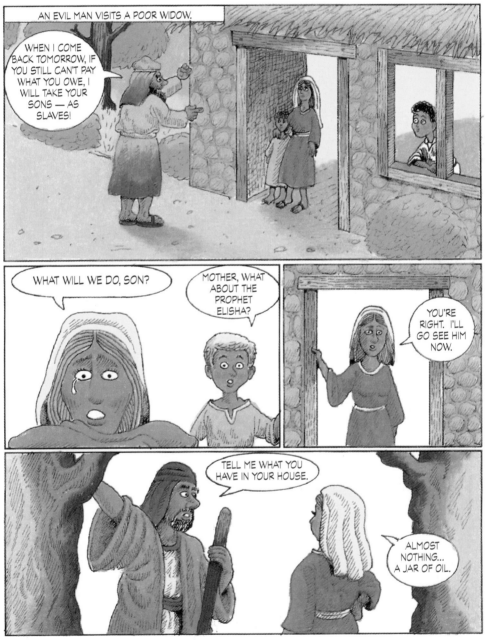

THEN HE SAID, GO, BORROW THEE VESSELS ABROAD OF ALL THY
NEIGHBOURS, EVEN EMPTY VESSELS; BORROW NOT A FEW.
2 KINGS 4:3

FOR THE LORD HAD MADE THE HOST OF THE SYRIANS TO HEAR A NOISE
OF CHARIOTS, AND A NOISE OF HORSES, EVEN THE NOISE
OF A GREAT HOST .... 2 KINGS 7:6

... ELISHA PRAYED UNTO THE LORD, AND SAID, SMITE THIS PEOPLE, I PRAY THEE, WITH BLINDNESS. AND HE SMOTE THEM WITH BLINDNESS ACCORDING TO THE WORD OF ELISHA.   2 KINGS 6:18

THE STORY OF KING JOSIAH

JOSIAH WAS EIGHT YEARS OLD WHEN HE BEGAN TO REIGN, . . . AND HE DID THAT WHICH WAS RIGHT IN THE SIGHT OF THE LORD, AND WALKED IN ALL THE WAY OF DAVID HIS FATHER . . . . **2 KINGS 22:1-2**

... AND LET THEM GIVE IT TO THE DOERS OF THE WORK WHICH IS IN THE HOUSE OF THE LORD, TO REPAIR THE BREACHES OF THE HOUSE, UNTO CARPENTERS, AND BUILDERS, AND MASONS, AND TO BUY TIMBER AND HEWN STONE TO REPAIR THE HOUSE.   2 KINGS 22:5-6

The Story of King Josiah 107 2 Kings 22

AND SHAPHAN THE SCRIBE SHEWED THE KING, SAYING, HILKIAH THE PRIEST HATH DELIVERED ME A BOOK. AND SHAPHAN READ IT BEFORE THE KING. **2 KINGS 22:10**

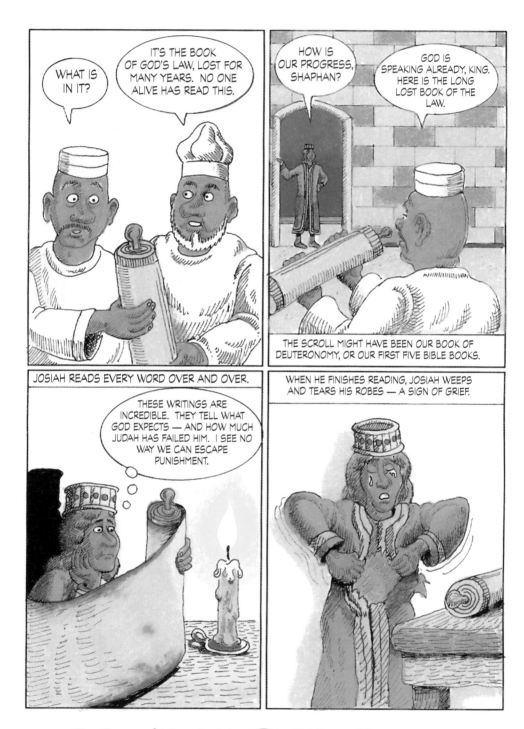

AND THE KING STOOD BY A PILLAR, AND MADE A COVENANT BEFORE THE
LORD, TO WALK AFTER THE LORD, AND TO KEEP HIS COMMANDMENTS
AND HIS TESTIMONIES AND HIS STATUTES WITH ALL THEIR HEART AND
ALL THEIR SOUL . . . .   2 KINGS 23:3

JOSIAH SENDS HIS MEN TO THE PROPHETESS HULDAH.

TELL JOSIAH GOD SAYS THIS: JUDAH MUST BE DESTROYED DUE TO ITS DISOBEDIENCE — BUT NOT WHILE JOSIAH IS ALIVE, BECAUSE HE HAS HONORED GOD.

PEOPLE OF ISRAEL, THIS IS THE LAW OF GOD FOUND IN THE TEMPLE. I WILL READ IT TO YOU, THEN MAKE SOME CHANGES.

THE KING ORDERS ALL IDOLS TO BE BURNED.

LORD, I KNOW EVIL DAYS ARE COMING. WE BROUGHT THEM ON OURSELVES. BUT IN MY TIME, I WILL DO ALL I CAN TO MAKE THIS A NATION WHICH PLEASES YOU.

The Story of King Josiah 109 2 Kings 22

EZRA: THE HOMECOMING

AND THEM THAT HAD ESCAPED FROM THE SWORD CARRIED HE AWAY TO BABYLON; WHERE THEY WERE SERVANTS TO HIM AND HIS SONS UNTIL THE REIGN OF THE KINGDOM OF PERSIA.   **2 CHRONICLES 36:20**

JOSIAH PROVES TO BE THE LAST GREAT KING OF JUDAH. AFTER HIS TIME, THE COUNTRY TURNS BACK TO IDOLS AND BECOMES WEAKER. IN 586 B.C., THE POWERFUL BABYLONIAN ARMY DESTROYS JERUSALEM AND CARRIES AWAY THE JEWS TO BABYLON.

FOR MANY YEARS THE JEWS ARE AWAY FROM THEIR TRUE HOME.

JERUSALEM WAS BEAUTIFUL. WE HAD A WONDERFUL TEMPLE FOR GOD.

MAYBE SOMEDAY I'LL GO THERE!

NEVER! GOD HAS FORGOTTEN US.

NO, THERE'S HOPE — BABYLON HAS FALLEN TO PERSIA, AND THEY SAY KING CYRUS WILL BE GOOD TO THE JEWS.

THUS SAITH CYRUS KING OF PERSIA, THE LORD GOD OF HEAVEN HATH GIVEN ME ALL THE KINGDOMS OF THE EARTH; AND HE HATH CHARGED ME TO BUILD HIM AN HOUSE AT JERUSALEM, WHICH IS IN JUDAH.

EZRA 1:2

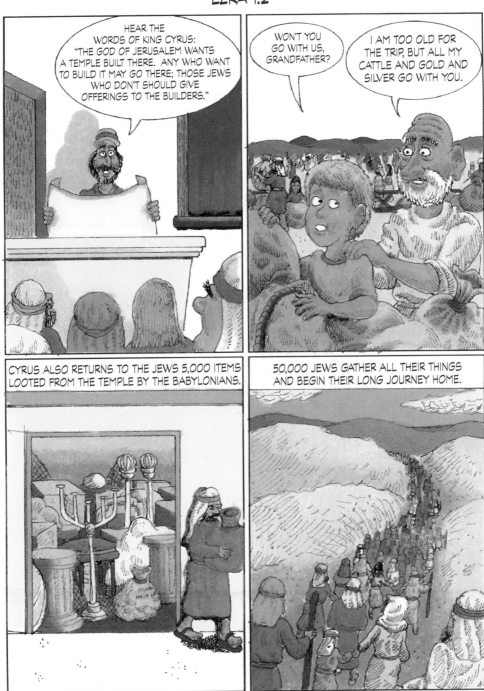

AND WHEN THE SEVENTH MONTH WAS COME, AND THE CHILDREN OF ISRAEL WERE IN THE CITIES, THE PEOPLE GATHERED THEMSELVES TOGETHER AS ONE MAN TO JERUSALEM.   **EZRA 3:1**

BLESSED BE THE LORD GOD OF OUR FATHERS, WHICH HATH PUT SUCH A THING AS THIS IN THE KING'S HEART, TO BEAUTIFY THE HOUSE OF THE LORD WHICH IS IN JERUSALEM.   EZRA 7:27

NEHEMIAH AND THE WALLS

AND IT CAME TO PASS, WHEN I HEARD THESE WORDS, THAT I SAT DOWN AND WEPT, AND MOURNED CERTAIN DAYS, AND FASTED, AND PRAYED BEFORE THE GOD OF HEAVEN.   NEHEMIAH 1:4

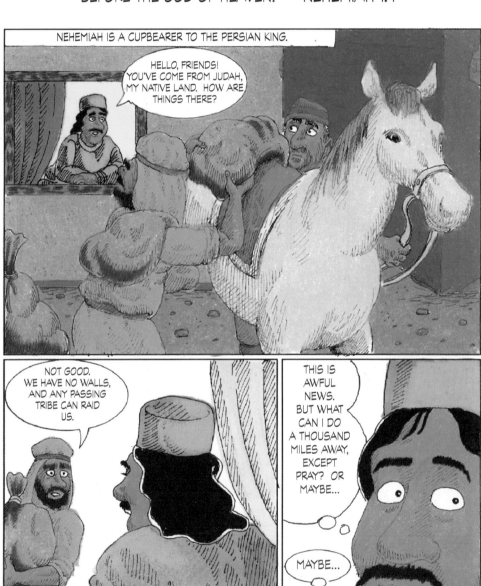

AND I SAID UNTO THE KING, IF IT PLEASE THE KING, AND IF THY SERVANT HAVE FOUND FAVOUR IN THY SIGHT, THAT THOU WOULDEST SEND ME UNTO JUDAH .... NEHEMIAH 2:5

THEN ANSWERED I THEM, AND SAID UNTO THEM, THE GOD OF HEAVEN, HE
WILL PROSPER US; THEREFORE WE HIS SERVANTS WILL
ARISE AND BUILD . . . .   NEHEMIAH 2:20

SO BUILT WE THE WALL; AND ALL THE WALL WAS JOINED TOGETHER
UNTO THE HALF THEREOF: FOR THE PEOPLE HAD A MIND TO WORK.
NEHEMIAH 4:6

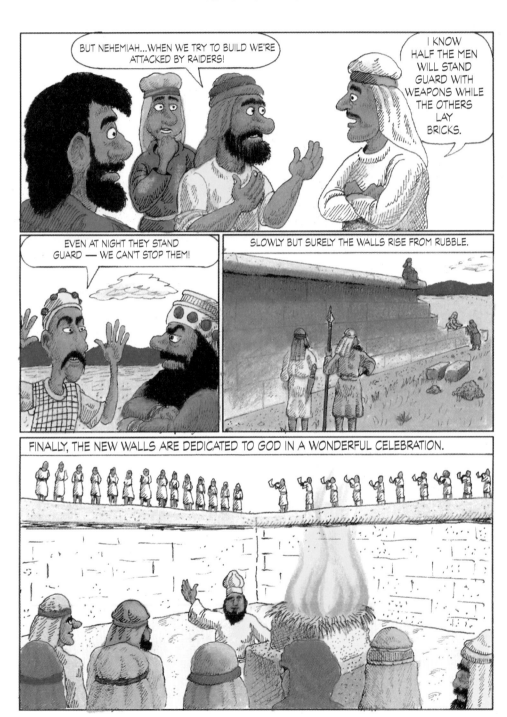

Nehemiah and the Walls Nehemiah

ESTHER THE QUEEN

AND THE KING LOVED ESTHER ABOVE ALL THE WOMEN, AND SHE OBTAINED GRACE AND FAVOUR IN HIS SIGHT ... SO THAT HE SET THE ROYAL CROWN UPON HER HEAD .... **ESTHER 2:17**

THIS IS A STORY FROM THE TIME OF THE PERSIAN EMPIRE, WHEN MANY JEWS LIVED FAR AWAY FROM HOME.

MY SEARCH FOR A QUEEN IS OVER. I CHOOSE ESTHER!

BUT THERE IS ONE THING THE KING DOESN'T KNOW ABOUT ESTHER.

MORDECAI SITS OUT BY THE PALACE GATE EACH DAY.

I HAVE TO TALK TO MY COUSIN ESTHER. MAYBE SHE'LL SEE ME HERE.

I'M THE ONLY ONE WHO KNOWS SHE IS JEWISH. WHAT WOULD THE KING SAY IF HE FOUND OUT?

AND ESTHER SAID, THE ADVERSARY AND ENEMY IS THIS WICKED HAMAN.
THEN HAMAN WAS AFRAID BEFORE THE KING AND THE QUEEN.
ESTHER 7:6

AND WHEN HAMAN SAW THAT MORDECAI BOWED NOT, NOR DID HIM
REVERENCE, THEN WAS HAMAN FULL OF WRATH.   ESTHER 3:5

THEN SAID THE KING UNTO HER, WHAT WILT THOU, QUEEN ESTHER? AND WHAT IS THY REQUEST? IT SHALL BE EVEN GIVEN THEE TO THE HALF OF THE KINGDOM.   **ESTHER 5:3**

THE STORY OF JOB

AND THE LORD SAID UNTO SATAN, HAST THOU CONSIDERED MY
SERVANT JOB, THAT THERE IS NONE LIKE HIM IN THE EARTH, A PERFECT
AND AN UPRIGHT MAN, ONE THAT FEARETH GOD . . . ?   JOB 1:8

AND THE LORD SAID UNTO SATAN, BEHOLD, ALL THAT HE HATH IS IN THY POWER; ONLY UPON HIMSELF PUT NOT FORTH THINE HAND. SO SATAN WENT FORTH FROM THE PRESENCE OF THE LORD. JOB 1:12

The Story of Job 123 Job

... WHAT? SHALL WE RECEIVE GOOD AT THE HAND OF GOD, AND SHALL
WE NOT RECEIVE EVIL? IN ALL THIS DID NOT JOB SIN WITH HIS LIPS.
JOB 2:10

AND THE LORD TURNED THE CAPTIVITY OF JOB, WHEN HE PRAYED FOR
HIS FRIENDS: ALSO THE LORD GAVE JOB TWICE AS MUCH
AS HE HAD BEFORE.   JOB 42:10

The Story Of Job 125 Job

SONGS AND WISDOM

THE LORD IS MY SHEPHERD; I SHALL NOT WANT. HE MAKETH ME TO LIE DOWN IN GREEN PASTURES . . . .   PSALM 23:1-2

ALONG WITH JOB, THE PSALMS, PROVERBS, ECCLESIASTES, AND SONG OF SONGS OFFER WISDOM, MUSIC, AND POETRY FOR GOD'S FAMILY.

PSALMS

THE PSALMS ARE SONGS TO AND ABOUT GOD. DAVID WROTE MANY OF THEM. PSALM 23 TELLS HOW GOD IS LIKE A GOOD SHEPHERD.

THE LORD IS MY SHEPHERD, I SHALL NOT WANT. HE MAKES ME LIKE DOWN IN GREEN PASTURES, HE LEADS ME BESIDE THE STILL WATERS, HE RESTORES MY SOUL...

EVEN THOUGH I WALK THROUGH THE VALLEY OF THE SHADOW OF DEATH, I WILL FEAR NO EVIL, FOR YOU ARE WITH ME, YOUR ROD AND YOUR STAFF, THEY COMFORT ME...

PSALM 1 DESCRIBES THE REWARDS OF OBEYING GOD.

BLESSED IS THE MAN WHO WALKS NOT IN THE COUNSEL OF THE UNGODLY, NOR STANDS IN THE WAY OF SINNERS... BUT HIS DELIGHT IS IN THE LAW OF THE LORD, AND HE MEDITATES ON IT DAY AND NIGHT. AND HE SHALL BE LIKE A TREE PLANTED BY THE RIVER, THAT BRINGS FORTH HIS FRUIT IN HIS SEASON...

MAKE A JOYFUL NOISE UNTO THE LORD, ALL YE LANDS. SERVE THE LORD
WITH GLADNESS: COME BEFORE HIS PRESENCE WITH SINGING.
PSALM 100:1-2

PSALM 100 CALLS FOR US TO WORSHIP AND PRAISE GOD TOGETHER.

MAKE A JOYFUL NOISE TO THE LORD,
ALL THE EARTH.
SERVE THE LORD WITH GLADNESS
COME BEFORE HIM WITH JOYFUL
SONGS,
KNOW THAT THE LORD IS GOD.
IT'S HE WHO MAKES US, AND NOT
WE OURSELVES.
WE ARE HIS PEOPLE, THE SHEEP OF
HIS PASTURE.
ENTER HIS GATES WITH THANKSGIVING
AND HIS COURTS WITH PRAISE...

IN PSALM 51, DAVID ASKS GOD TO CLEANSE HIM OF HIS SIN.

...CREATE IN ME A CLEAN
HEART, O GOD; RENEW
A RIGHT SPIRIT WITHIN ME.
CAST ME NOT AWAY FROM YOUR
PRESENCE; AND TAKE NOT
YOUR HOLY SPIRIT FROM ME.

RESTORE UNTO ME THE JOY OF
YOUR SALVATION...

O LORD, OPEN MY LIPS,
AND MY MOUTH WILL DECLARE
YOUR PRAISE...

PSALM 8 CELEBRATES THE BEAUTY OF GOD'S CREATION.

O LORD, OUR LORD,
HOW MAJESTIC IS YOUR NAME
IN ALL THE EARTH...

WHEN I CONSIDER THE HEAVENS,
THE WORK OF YOUR FINGERS,
THE MOON AND THE STARS
WHICH YOU SET IN PLACE,
WHAT IS MAN, THAT YOU ARE MINDFUL
OF HIM?...

O LORD, OUR LORD, HOW EXCELLENT
IS YOUR NAME IN ALL THE EARTH!

TO KNOW WISDOM AND INSTRUCTION; TO PERCEIVE THE WORDS OF UNDERSTANDING; TO RECEIVE THE INSTRUCTION OF WISDOM, JUSTICE, AND JUDGMENT, AND EQUITY.   PROVERBS 1:2-3

THE PROVERBS OFFER WISE ADVICE FOR EVERYDAY LIVING. SOLOMON WROTE MANY OF THEM.

THE FEAR OF THE LORD IS THE BEGINNING OF WISDOM. (1:7)

A GOSSIP BETRAYS A CONFIDENCE, BUT A TRUSTWORTHY MAN KEEPS A SECRET. (11:13)

TRUST IN THE LORD WITH ALL YOUR HEART, AND LEAN NOT ON YOUR OWN UNDERSTANDING. IN ALL YOUR WAYS ACKNOWLEDGE HIM, AND HE WILL MAKE STRAIGHT YOUR PATH. (3:5-6)

BLESSED IS HE WHO IS KIND TO THE NEEDY. (14:21)

A HAPPY HEART MAKES A CHEERFUL FACE. (15:13)

A GENTLE ANSWER TURNS AWAY WRATH, BUT A HARSH WORD STIRS UP ANGER. (15:1)

A FRIEND LOVES AT ALL TIMES. (17:17)

TRAIN A CHILD IN THE WAY HE SHOULD GO, AND WHEN HE IS OLDER HE WILL NOT DEPART FROM IT. (22:6)

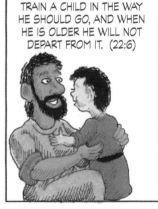

LAZINESS BRINGS ON DEEP SLEEP, AND THE SHIFTLESS MAN GOES HUNGRY. (19:15)

LET US HEAR THE CONCLUSION OF THE WHOLE MATTER: FEAR GOD, AND KEEP HIS COMMANDMENTS: FOR THIS IS THE WHOLE DUTY OF MAN.
ECCLESIASTES 12:13

WHY IS LIFE SO OFTEN UNHAPPY? THE WRITER OF ECCLESIASTES SHOWS THAT OBEYING GOD MAKES LIFE MEANINGFUL.

THERE IS A TIME FOR EVERYTHING, AND A SEASON UNDER HEAVEN FOR EVERY ACTIVITY.

A TIME TO BE BORN, AND
A TIME TO DIE,
A TIME TO PLANT AND
A TIME TO UPROOT...
A TIME TO WEEP AND
A TIME TO LAUGH...
A TIME TO BE SILENT AND
A TIME TO SPEAK...
A TIME FOR WAR AND
A TIME FOR PEACE...
(FROM CHAPTER 3)

NOW IT HAS ALL BEEN HEARD; HERE IS THE CONCLUSION: FEAR GOD AND KEEP HIS COMMANDMENTS, FOR THIS IS THE WHOLE DUTY OF MAN. (12:13)

THE SONG OF SONGS SHOWS THE LOVE BETWEEN HUSBAND AND WIFE — AND OUR LOVE TO GOD.

LOVE BURNS LIKE
A ROARING FIRE,
LIKE A MIGHTY FLAME.
MANY WATERS
CANNOT QUENCH LOVE;
RIVERS CANNOT WASH
IT AWAY.

IF ONE WERE TO GIVE
ALL THE WEALTH
OF ONE'S HOUSE FOR LOVE,
IT WOULD BE COMPLETELY
SCORNED.

ISAIAH AND JEREMIAH

ALSO I HEARD THE VOICE OF THE LORD, SAYING, WHOM SHALL I SEND,
AND WHO WILL GO FOR US? THEN SAID I, HERE AM I; SEND ME.
ISAIAH 6:8

FOR UNTO US A CHILD IS BORN, UNTO US A SON IS GIVEN: AND THE GOVERNMENT SHALL BE UPON HIS SHOULDER: AND HIS NAME SHALL BE CALLED WONDERFUL, COUNSELLOR . . . .   ISAIAH **9:6**

BUT ISAIAH PREDICTS A WONDERFUL TIME AHEAD WHEN A SPECIAL CHILD WILL ENTER THE WORLD.

"THE PEOPLE WALKING IN DARKNESS HAVE SEEN A GREAT LIGHT...."

"FOR UNTO US A CHILD IS BORN, UNTO US A SON IS GIVEN."

"AND HE WILL BE CALLED WONDERFUL, COUNSELOR, MIGHTY GOD, EVERLASTING FATHER, THE PRINCE OF PEACE."

BUT ISAIAH ALSO SEES OTHER THINGS FOR THIS "MESSIAH."

"... A MAN OF SORROWS, AND FAMILIAR WITH SUFFERING — DESPISED AND REJECTED BY MEN."

"PIERCED FOR OUR SINS. AND BY HIS WOUNDS WE ARE HEALED."

700 YEARS BEFORE JESUS, ISAIAH GIVES A CLEAR PICTURE OF HIM!

BEFORE I FORMED THEE IN THE BELLY I KNEW THEE; AND BEFORE THOU CAMEST FORTH OUT OF THE WOMB I SANCTIFIED THEE, AND I ORDAINED THEE A PROPHET UNTO THE NATIONS.   **JEREMIAH 1:5**

THE HEART IS DECEITFUL ABOVE ALL THINGS, AND DESPERATELY WICKED:
WHO CAN KNOW IT?   JEREMIAH 17:9

THE STORY OF EZEKIEL

AND I LOOKED, AND, BEHOLD, A WHIRLWIND CAME OUT OF THE NORTH, A
GREAT CLOUD, AND A FIRE INFOLDING ITSELF, AND A BRIGHTNESS
WAS ABOUT IT . . . .   EZEKIEL 1:4

AND WHEN THEY WENT, I HEARD THE NOISE OF THEIR WINGS, LIKE THE NOISE OF GREAT WATERS, AS THE VOICE OF THE ALMIGHTY, THE VOICE OF SPEECH, AS THE NOISE OF AN HOST . . . .   EZEKIEL 1:24

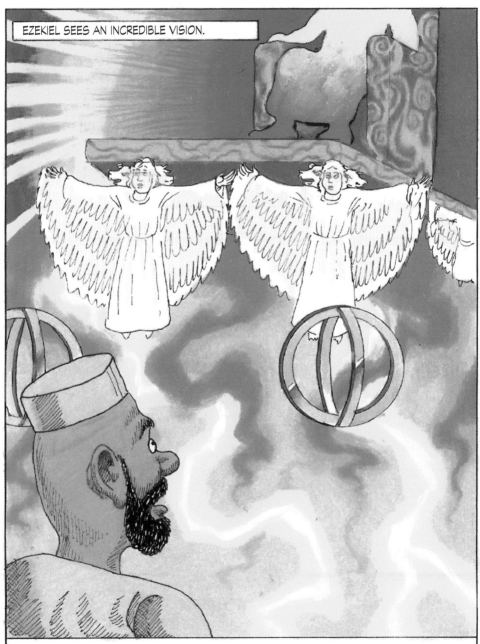

EZEKIEL SEES AN INCREDIBLE VISION.

EACH PART OF THE VISION — THE ANIMALS, THE WHEELS, THE THRONE — HAS A MESSAGE FOR EZEKIEL ABOUT THE POWER AND GLORY OF GOD.

THE HAND OF THE LORD WAS UPON ME, AND CARRIED ME OUT IN THE SPIRIT OF THE LORD, AND SET ME DOWN IN THE MIDST OF THE VALLEY WHICH WAS FULL OF BONES.   EZEKIEL 37:1

SO I PROPHESIED AS HE COMMANDED ME, AND THE BREATH CAME INTO THEM, AND THEY LIVED, AND STOOD UP UPON THEIR FEET, AN EXCEEDING GREAT ARMY.   EZEKIEL 37:10

EZEKIEL HEARS A RATTLING. THE BONES BEGIN CONNECTING AND REJOINING.

SOON, A MIGHTY ARMY STANDS BEFORE HIM!

THESE BONES ARE ISRAEL! IT MEANS WE'LL RETURN TO LIFE AND POWER JUST LIKE THESE BONES!

The Story of Ezekiel   137   Ezekiel

THE STORY OF DANIEL

... THESE MEN, O KING, HAVE NOT REGARDED THEE: THEY SERVE NOT THY GODS, NOR WORSHIP THE GOLDEN IMAGE WHICH THOU HAST SET UP.
DANIEL 3:12

DURING THE JEWS' CAPTIVITY IN BABYLON, FAR FROM HOME, DANIEL AND THREE FRIENDS — SHADRACH, MESHACH, AND ABEDNEGO — HOLD IMPORTANT JOBS UNDER THE KING, WHO HOLDS THEM IN RESPECT.

HOW CAN WE BE TRUE TO GOD WHILE SERVING AN UNBELIEVING KING?

JUST HAVE FAITH AND OBEY THE LORD.

KING NEBUCHADNEZZAR ISSUES AN ORDER.

KING NEBUCHADNEZZAR ORDERS EVERYONE TO BOW BEFORE THIS NEW IDOL.

KING, THREE MEN — ALL HEBREWS — REFUSED TO KNEEL!

WHAT'S THIS? I EXPECT MY LEADERS TO OBEY ME! SUMMON THEM!

HE ANSWERED AND SAID, LO, I SEE FOUR MEN LOOSE, WALKING IN THE MIDST OF THE FIRE, AND THEY HAVE NO HURT; AND THE FORM OF THE FOURTH IS LIKE THE SON OF GOD.   **DANIEL 3:25**

The Story of Daniel   (140)   Daniel

MY GOD HATH SENT HIS ANGEL, AND HATH SHUT THE LIONS' MOUTHS, THAT THEY HAVE NOT HURT ME: FORASMUCH AS BEFORE HIM INNOCENCY WAS FOUND IN ME . . . .   DANIEL 6:22

The Story of Daniel   141   Daniel

THE STORY OF JONAH

ARISE, GO TO NINEVEH, THAT GREAT CITY, AND CRY AGAINST IT; FOR
THEIR WICKEDNESS IS COME UP BEFORE ME.   JONAH 1:2

SO THEY TOOK UP JONAH, AND CAST HIM FORTH INTO THE SEA: AND THE
SEA CEASED FROM HER RAGING.   JONAH 1:15

AND [JONAH] SAID, I CRIED BY REASON OF MINE AFFLICTION UNTO THE LORD, AND HE HEARD ME; OUT OF THE BELLY OF HELL CRIED I, AND THOU HEARDEST MY VOICE.   JONAH 2:2

BUT LET MAN AND BEAST BE COVERED WITH SACKCLOTH, AND CRY MIGHTILY UNTO GOD: YEA, LET THEM TURN EVERY ONE FROM HIS EVIL WAY, AND FROM THE VIOLENCE THAT IS IN THEIR HANDS.   JONAH 3:8

THE KING ISSUES A COMMAND.

NO ONE IN THIS CITY — NOT EVEN THE ANIMALS — SHALL EAT OR DRINK. EVERYONE IS TO CALL ON GOD'S NAME. IF WE TURN FROM OUR EVIL, PERHAPS GOD WILL SPARE US.
—BY ORDER OF THE KING

SO GOD SPARES THE CITY.

YET JONAH IS NOT PLEASED.

I KNEW THIS WOULD HAPPEN, LORD. YOU ARE SO MERCIFUL YOU'LL EVEN SPARE THESE ENEMIES OF THE JEWS. YOU MIGHT FORGIVE THEM — BUT I CAN'T.

HE STAYS AND WATCHES, THINKING GOD MIGHT STILL DESTROY NINEVEH.

GOD TEACHES JONAH A LESSON: HE MAKES THE VINE OVER JONAH'S HEAD WITHER.

MY SHADE IS GONE... I'M DYING OF THE HEAT.

TAKE MY LIFE, LORD...

PLEASE!

JONAH, YOU'RE CONCERNED ABOUT A VINE YOU DIDN'T CREATE. SHOULDN'T I CARE ABOUT A CITY FULL OF HELPLESS PEOPLE AND ANIMALS?

The Story of Jonah 145 Jonah

THE MINOR PROPHETS

ALAS FOR THE DAY! FOR THE DAY OF THE LORD IS AT HAND, AND AS A DESTRUCTION FROM THE ALMIGHTY SHALL IT COME.   **JOEL 1:15**

TWELVE MEN, INCLUDING JONAH, ARE KNOWN AS MINOR PROPHETS ONLY BECAUSE THE OTHER PROPHETS — ISAIAH, JEREMIAH, EZEKIEL, AND DANIEL — WROTE LONGER BOOKS.

REPENT! TURN BACK TO GOD!

GOD CHOSE THESE MEN TO SPEAK TO JUDAH AND ISRAEL FOR HIM.

HOSEA IS A STORY OF LOVE AND FORGIVENESS. JUST AS THE PROPHET ACCEPTS A WIFE WHO HAS FAILED HIM, SO WILL GOD RESTORE AND FORGIVE ISRAEL.

JOEL WARNS OF THE DAY OF THE LORD, JUDGMENT DAY. BUT HE ALSO PREDICTS A DAY WHEN GOD WILL POUR OUT HIS SPIRIT ON ALL PEOPLE.

THE LORD'S VOICE CRIETH UNTO THE CITY, AND THE MAN OF WISDOM
SHALL SEE THY NAME: HEAR YE THE ROD, AND WHO HATH APPOINTED IT.
MICAH 6:9

AMOS IS A SHEPHERD PREACHING ABOUT JUSTICE. HE WARNS THAT GOD CARES
HOW WE TREAT THE POOR.

PREPARE TO MEET OUR GOD!

OBADIAH HAS A WARNING FOR EDOM. THAT NEIGHBOR REFUSED TO HELP THE JEWS
WHEN JERUSALEM WAS BEING DESTROYED. SO GOD WILL BRING JUDGMENT.

MICAH SPEAKS FOR THE POOR, LIKE AMOS. HE PREACHES AGAINST THEIR MISTREATMENT.
BUT HE ALSO PREDICTS THAT A WONDERFUL CHILD WILL BE BORN IN BETHLEHEM.

THEREFORE THE LAW IS SLACKED, AND JUDGMENT DOTH NEVER GO FORTH: FOR THE WICKED DOTH COMPASS ABOUT THE RIGHTEOUS; THEREFORE WRONG JUDGMENT PROCEEDETH.   HABAKKUK 1:4

NAHUM FOLLOWS IN JONAH'S STEPS, PREACHING IN NINEVEH 150 YEARS LATER.

THEY HAVE ANGERED GOD AGAIN, AND THIS TIME IT MEANS THEIR DESTRUCTION AT THE HANDS OF BABYLON.

HABAKKUK ASKS GOD WHY EVIL PEOPLE GO UNPUNISHED. GOD ANSWERS THAT HE WILL INDEED PUNISH THE WICKED.

"THE LORD IS IN HIS HOLY TEMPLE. LET ALL THE EARTH KEEP SILENT BEFORE HIM."

ZEPHANIAH IS A COUSIN OF KING JOSIAH, WHO BRINGS REVIVAL TO JUDAH. THIS PROPHET HELPS SPREAD THE WORD TO RETURN TO GOD.

REMEMBER YE THE LAW OF MOSES MY SERVANT, WHICH I COMMANDED
UNTO HIM IN HOREB FOR ALL ISRAEL, WITH THE STATUTES
AND JUDGMENTS.   MALACHI 4:4

HAGGAI HAS A PRACTICAL MESSAGE: BUILD THE TEMPLE! AFTER THE RETURN FROM
BABYLON, THIS PROPHET ENCOURAGES THE PEOPLE TO RESTORE THE HOUSE OF GOD.

ZECHARIAH, LIKE HIS FRIEND HAGGAI, PREACHES ABOUT THE TEMPLE — AND OF THE
DAY WHEN THE MESSIAH WILL ENTER JERUSALEM RIDING A YOUNG DONKEY.

MALACHI CLOSES THE OLD TESTAMENT. TO THOSE WHOSE FAITH HAS DIED, MALACHI
SAYS, "GIVE GOD YOUR BEST!"

BUT THE PEOPLE ARE
FURTHER FROM GOD
THAN EVER BEFORE—AND
FOR 400 YEARS HE
WILL BE SILENT.

THE BIRTH OF JESUS

AND MARY SAID, MY SOUL DOTH MAGNIFY THE LORD, AND MY SPIRIT HATH REJOICED IN GOD MY SAVIOUR.   LUKE 1:46-47

AND JOSEPH ALSO WENT UP FROM GALILEE, OUT OF THE CITY OF
NAZARETH, INTO JUDAEA, UNTO THE CITY OF DAVID,
WHICH IS CALLED BETHLEHEM.   LUKE 2:4

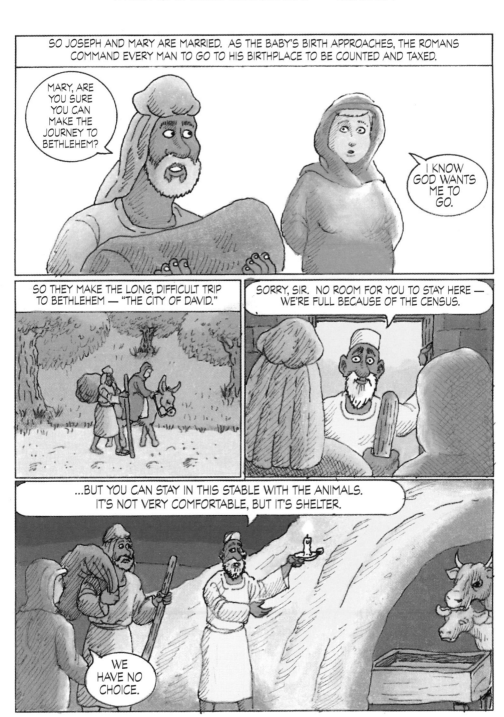

AND SHE BROUGHT FORTH HER FIRSTBORN SON, AND WRAPPED HIM IN SWADDLING CLOTHES, AND LAID HIM IN A MANGER; BECAUSE THERE WAS NO ROOM FOR THEM IN THE INN.   LUKE 2:7

THAT NIGHT MARY GIVES BIRTH TO A SON, AND NAMES HIM JESUS AS THE ANGEL SAID.

NEARBY SHEPHERDS WATCH THEIR FLOCK.

DON'T BE AFRAID — I BRING GOOD NEWS FOR EVERYONE! TODAY, IN DAVID'S CITY, A BABY IS BORN — A SAVIOR WHO IS CHRIST THE LORD. YOU WILL FIND HIM LYING IN A MANGER.

SUDDENLY THE SKY IS FILLED WITH ANGELS, ALL OF THEM SINGING AND PRAISING GOD.

GLORY TO GOD IN THE HIGHEST! AND ON EARTH, PEACE, GOOD WILL TO MEN!

AND SUDDENLY THERE WAS WITH THE ANGEL A MULTITUDE OF THE
HEAVENLY HOST PRAISING GOD, AND SAYING, GLORY TO GOD IN THE
HIGHEST, AND ON EARTH PEACE, GOOD WILL TOWARD MEN.
LUKE 2:13-14

LET'S GO SEE THIS AMAZING CHILD!
BETHLEHEM IS JUST AHEAD.

THE TOWN IS QUIET, BUT THEY SEE THE
LIGHT FROM A STABLE.

THERE THEY FIND MARY, JOSEPH, AND A BEAUTIFUL CHILD.

LATER THE
SHEPHERDS
PRAISE GOD AS
THEY TELL
EVERYONE WHAT
THEY HAVE SEEN.

The Birth of Jesus ⟨153⟩ Luke 1 and 2

THE CHILDHOOD OF JESUS

... WHERE IS HE THAT IS BORN KING OF THE JEWS? FOR WE HAVE SEEN
HIS STAR IN THE EAST, AND ARE COME TO WORSHIP HIM.
MATTHEW 2:2

The Childhood of Jesus (154) Matthew 2 and Luke 2

AND WHEN THEY WERE COME INTO THE HOUSE, THEY SAW THE YOUNG CHILD WITH MARY HIS MOTHER, AND FELL DOWN, AND WORSHIPPED HIM: . . .THEY PRESENTED UNTO HIM GIFTS; GOLD, AND FRANKINCENSE, AND MYRRH.   MATTHEW 2:11

The Childhood of Jesus (155) Matthew 2 and Luke 2

NOW HIS PARENTS WENT TO JERUSALEM EVERY YEAR AT THE FEAST OF THE PASSOVER. AND WHEN HE WAS TWELVE YEARS OLD, THEY WENT UP TO JERUSALEM AFTER THE CUSTOM OF THE FEAST.   LUKE 2:41-42

AND HE SAID UNTO THEM, HOW IS IT THAT YE SOUGHT ME? WIST YE
NOT THAT I MUST BE ABOUT MY FATHER'S BUSINESS?   LUKE 2:49

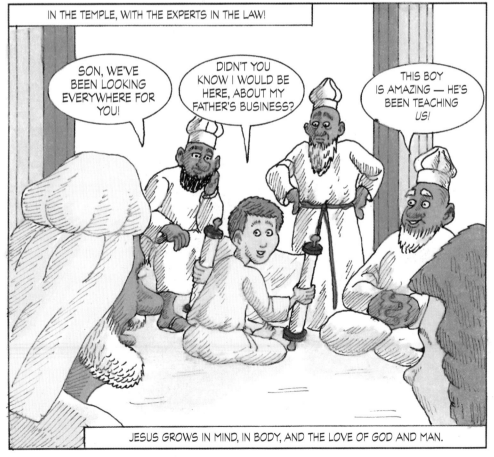

The Childhood of Jesus   157   Matthew 2 and Luke 2

THE BAPTISM OF JESUS

AND HE CAME INTO ALL THE COUNTRY ABOUT JORDAN, PREACHING THE BAPTISM OF REPENTANCE FOR THE REMISSION OF SINS.   LUKE 3:3

AS HE GROWS TO MANHOOD IN NAZARETH, JESUS IS OFTEN FOUND IN THE SYNAGOGUE.

THE PROPHET ISAIAH SAYS, "THE SPIRIT OF THE LORD IS ON ME, BECAUSE HE HAS PREPARED ME TO PREACH GOOD NEWS FOR THE POOR..."

TODAY, BEFORE YOUR VERY EYES, THOSE WORDS ARE COMING TRUE.

ISN'T THIS JOSEPH'S SON?

HE SEEMS CONFIDENT IN HIMSELF.

... I INDEED BAPTIZE YOU WITH WATER; BUT ONE MIGHTIER
THAN I COMETH, THE LATCHET OF WHOSE SHOES I AM NOT WORTHY
TO UNLOOSE .... LUKE 3:16

AND THE HOLY GHOST DESCENDED IN A BODILY SHAPE LIKE A DOVE
UPON HIM, AND A VOICE CAME FROM HEAVEN, WHICH SAID, THOU ART
MY BELOVED SON; IN THEE I AM WELL PLEASED.   LUKE **3:22**

The Baptism of Jesus   (161) Luke **3**

JESUS IS TEMPTED

AND JESUS BEING FULL OF THE HOLY GHOST RETURNED FROM JORDAN,
AND WAS LED BY THE SPIRIT INTO THE WILDERNESS.   LUKE 4:1

JESUS, FILLED WITH THE SPIRIT OF GOD, RETURNS FROM JORDAN.

THE SAME SPIRIT IMMEDIATELY LEADS JESUS DEEP INTO THE DESERT.

FOR 40 DAYS, HE IS ALONE IN THE DESERT. HAVING EATEN NOTHING, HE GROWS HUNGRY.

AND JESUS ANSWERED AND SAID UNTO HIM, GET THEE BEHIND ME, SATAN: FOR IT IS WRITTEN, THOU SHALT WORSHIP THE LORD THY GOD, AND HIM ONLY SHALT THOU SERVE.   LUKE 4:8

AND JESUS ANSWERING SAID UNTO HIM, IT IS SAID, THOU SHALT NOT TEMPT THE LORD THY GOD. AND WHEN THE DEVIL HAD ENDED ALL THE TEMPTATION, HE DEPARTED FROM HIM FOR A SEASON.   LUKE 4:12-13

AND THEY WERE ALL AMAZED ... AND THE FAME OF HIM WENT OUT INTO EVERY PLACE OF THE COUNTRY ROUND ABOUT.   LUKE 4:36-37

JESUS FINDS DISCIPLES

AND HE ENTERED INTO ONE OF THE SHIPS, WHICH WAS SIMON'S, . . . AND HE SAT DOWN, AND TAUGHT THE PEOPLE OUT OF THE SHIP.   LUKE **5:3**

NOW WHEN HE HAD LEFT SPEAKING, HE SAID UNTO SIMON, LAUNCH OUT
INTO THE DEEP, AND LET DOWN YOUR NETS FOR A DRAUGHT.
LUKE 5:4

AND WHEN IT WAS DAY, HE CALLED UNTO HIM HIS DISCIPLES: AND OF THEM HE CHOSE TWELVE, WHOM ALSO HE NAMED APOSTLES.
LUKE 6:13

Jesus Finds Disciples (168) Luke 5 and John 3

FOR GOD SO LOVED THE WORLD, THAT HE GAVE HIS ONLY BEGOTTEN SON, THAT WHOSOEVER BELIEVETH IN HIM SHOULD NOT PERISH, BUT HAVE EVERLASTING LIFE.   JOHN 3:16

JESUS TEACHES PEOPLE

AND SEEING THE MULTITUDES, HE WENT UP INTO A MOUNTAIN: AND WHEN HE WAS SET, HIS DISCIPLES CAME UNTO HIM.   MATTHEW 5:1

CROWDS BEGIN TO FOLLOW JESUS WHEREVER HE GOES. SO, AT THE MOUNTAINSIDE, HE SITS AND BEGINS TO TEACH HIS DISCIPLES.

BLESSED ARE THE POOR IN SPIRIT, FOR THEIRS IS THE KINGDOM OF HEAVEN. BLESSED ARE THOSE WHO MOURN, FOR THEY WILL BE COMFORTED.

THESE TEACHINGS ARE KNOWN AS THE SERMON ON THE MOUNT OR THE BEATITUDES.

LET YOUR LIGHT SO SHINE BEFORE MEN, THAT THEY MAY SEE YOUR
GOOD WORKS, AND GLORIFY YOUR FATHER WHICH IS IN HEAVEN.
MATTHEW 5:16

"YOU ARE THE SALT OF THE EARTH,"
HE CONTINUES.

SALT MAKES PEOPLE THIRSTY — AND
JESUS BRINGS LIVING WATER.

"YOU ARE THE LIGHT OF THE WORLD.
A CITY ON A HILL IS EASY TO SEE —
SO LET YOUR LIGHT SHINE BEFORE MEN."

"YOU'VE HEARD IT IS WRONG TO KILL
PEOPLE. BUT I SAY WHEN YOU BURN
WITH ANGER, IT IS LIKE MURDER."

"YOU'VE HEARD 'AN EYE FOR AN EYE.' BUT
I TELL YOU NOT TO FIGHT EVIL WITH
EVIL. IF SOMEONE STRIKES YOU ON
THE CHEEK, OFFER THE OTHER ONE."

BUT WHEN YE PRAY, USE NOT VAIN REPETITIONS, AS THE HEATHEN DO: FOR THEY THINK THAT THEY SHALL BE HEARD FOR THEIR MUCH SPEAKING.   MATTHEW 6:7

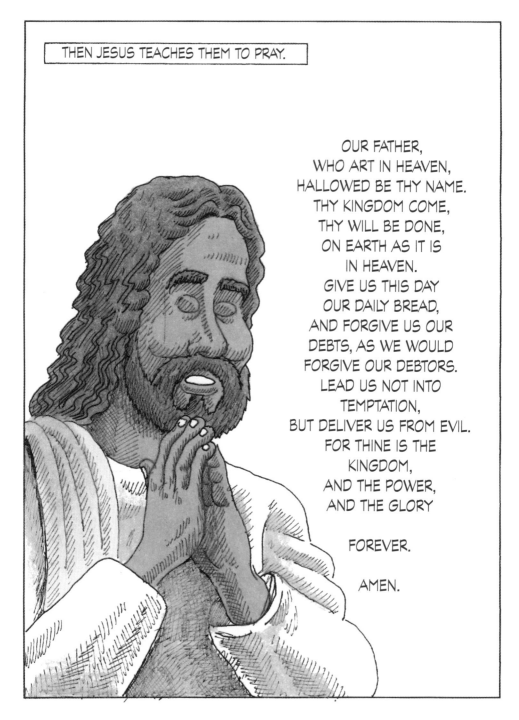

THEN JESUS TEACHES THEM TO PRAY.

OUR FATHER,
WHO ART IN HEAVEN,
HALLOWED BE THY NAME.
THY KINGDOM COME,
THY WILL BE DONE,
ON EARTH AS IT IS
IN HEAVEN.
GIVE US THIS DAY
OUR DAILY BREAD,
AND FORGIVE US OUR
DEBTS, AS WE WOULD
FORGIVE OUR DEBTORS.
LEAD US NOT INTO
TEMPTATION,
BUT DELIVER US FROM EVIL.
FOR THINE IS THE
KINGDOM,
AND THE POWER,
AND THE GLORY

FOREVER.

AMEN.

THEREFORE WHOSOEVER HEARETH THESE SAYINGS OF MINE, AND DOETH THEM, I WILL LIKEN HIM UNTO A WISE MAN, WHICH BUILT HIS HOUSE UPON A ROCK.   MATTHEW 7:24

JESUS TEACHES ABOUT WORRYING.

"DON'T WORRY ABOUT WHAT YOU'LL EAT OR WEAR. LIFE IS MORE IMPORTANT THAN FOOD OR CLOTHING. LOOK AT THE BIRDS: THEY DON'T WORRY, YET SOLOMON IN ALL HIS GLORY WASN'T DRESSED AS BEAUTIFULLY."

"AND DO NOT JUDGE OTHERS. GOD WILL JUDGE YOU JUST THE WAY YOU JUDGE OTHERS."

"IF YOU LISTEN TO THESE WORDS AND FOLLOW THEM, YOU'RE LIKE A MAN WHO BUILDS HIS HOUSE ON THE ROCK — IT WILL STAND AGAINST WIND AND STORMS. BUT IF YOU IGNORE MY WORDS, YOU'RE LIKE THE MAN WHO BUILT HIS HOUSE ON THE SAND. WHEN THE WIND AND STORMS CAME, HIS HOUSE FELL WITH A CRASH."

JESUS HEALS PEOPLE

... DAUGHTER, BE OF GOOD COMFORT; THY FAITH HATH MADE THEE
WHOLE. AND THE WOMAN WAS MADE WHOLE FROM THAT HOUR.
MATTHEW 9:22

AND WHEN HE SAW THEM, HE SAID UNTO THEM, GO SHEW YOURSELVES UNTO THE PRIESTS. AND IT CAME TO PASS, THAT, AS THEY WENT, THEY WERE CLEANSED.   LUKE 17:14

... THEY UNCOVERED THE ROOF WHERE HE WAS: AND WHEN THEY HAD BROKEN IT UP, THEY LET DOWN THE BED WHEREIN THE SICK OF THE PALSY LAY.   MARK 2:4

BUT THE MEN ARE DETERMINED, SO THEY CLIMB TO THE ROOF AND LOWER THE SICK MAN THROUGH AN OPENING.

I SAY UNTO THEE, ARISE, AND TAKE UP THY BED, AND GO THY WAY INTO THINE HOUSE. AND IMMEDIATELY HE AROSE, TOOK UP THE BED, AND WENT FORTH BEFORE THEM ALL . . . .   MARK 2:11-12

JESUS AND THE CHILDREN

THEN WERE THERE BROUGHT UNTO HIM LITTLE CHILDREN, THAT HE SHOULD PUT HIS HANDS ON THEM, AND PRAY: AND THE DISCIPLES REBUKED THEM.   MATTHEW 19:13

AS THE WORD SPREADS OF JESUS' HEALING POWER, THE CROWDS GROW. IT SEEMS THAT EVERYONE WANTS TO BE WITH JESUS.

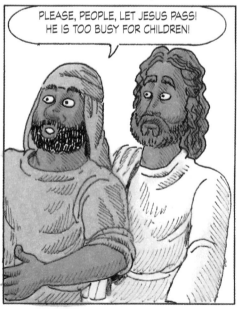

BUT JESUS SAID, SUFFER LITTLE CHILDREN, AND FORBID THEM NOT, TO
COME UNTO ME: FOR OF SUCH IS THE KINGDOM OF HEAVEN.
MATTHEW 19:14

LET THE LITTLE CHILDREN COME TO ME. DON'T BLOCK THEM — THE KINGDOM OF GOD BELONGS TO THEIR TYPE.

HERE'S THE TRUTH: ANYONE WHO DOESN'T RECEIVE GOD'S KINGDOM LIKE ONE OF THESE CHILDREN WILL NEVER ENTER IT.

FROM A MOUNTAINSIDE JESUS SEES A CROWD OF 5,000 PEOPLE GATHERING.

PHILIP, WHERE CAN WE BUY BREAD FOR A CROWD LIKE THIS?

YOU COULD WORK 8 MONTHS AND NOT EARN ENOUGH TO FEED THEM!

Jesus and the Children (179) Mark 10 and John 6

THERE IS A LAD HERE, WHICH HATH FIVE BARLEY LOAVES, AND TWO SMALL FISHES: BUT WHAT ARE THEY AMONG SO MANY?   JOHN 6:9

THEN THOSE MEN, WHEN THEY HAD SEEN THE MIRACLE THAT JESUS DID, SAID, THIS IS OF A TRUTH THAT PROPHET THAT SHOULD COME INTO THE WORLD.   JOHN 6:14

MIRACULOUSLY, 5,000 PEOPLE EAT THEIR FULL!

LET'S NOT WASTE. GATHER WHAT IS LEFT.

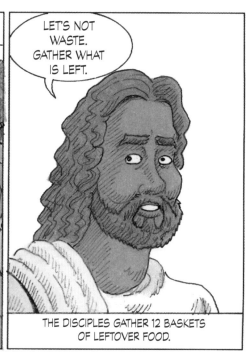

THE DISCIPLES GATHER 12 BASKETS OF LEFTOVER FOOD.

CAN YOU BELIEVE WHAT HAPPENED?

THIS IS THE KING FROM THE OLD PROPHECIES! WE'LL RAISE AN ARMY AND OVERPOWER THE ROMANS!

BUT JESUS IS NOT INTERESTED IN KINGS AND ARMIES, AND HE GOES TO THE MOUNTAIN ALONE.

Jesus and the Children   181   Mark 10 and John 6

JESUS WALKS ON WATER

AND WHEN HE HAD SENT THE MULTITUDES AWAY, HE WENT UP INTO A
MOUNTAIN APART TO PRAY: AND WHEN THE EVENING WAS COME,
HE WAS THERE ALONE.   MATTHEW 14:23

JESUS HAS FED 5,000, AND NOW HE INSTRUCTS HIS DISCIPLES.

TAKE THE BOAT
AND GO TO THE OTHER
SHORE WHILE I DISMISS
THESE PEOPLE.

WHEN EVERYONE IS GONE, JESUS GOES TO THE MOUNTAINSIDE TO SPEND TIME ALONE
WITH GOD.

BUT THE SHIP WAS NOW IN THE MIDST OF THE SEA, TOSSED WITH WAVES: FOR THE WIND WAS CONTRARY.   MATTHEW 14:24

AND WHEN THE DISCIPLES SAW HIM WALKING ON THE SEA, THEY WERE
TROUBLED, SAYING, IT IS A SPIRIT; AND THEY CRIED OUT FOR FEAR.
MATTHEW 14:26

AND IMMEDIATELY JESUS STRETCHED FORTH HIS HAND, AND CAUGHT HIM, AND SAID UNTO HIM, O THOU OF LITTLE FAITH, WHEREFORE DIDST THOU DOUBT?   MATTHEW 14:31

JESUS TELLS PARABLES

. . . A CERTAIN MAN WENT DOWN FROM JERUSALEM TO JERICHO, AND FELL AMONG THIEVES, WHICH STRIPPED HIM OF HIS RAIMENT, AND WOUNDED HIM, AND DEPARTED.   LUKE 10:30

JESUS TEACHES ABOUT GOD BY TELLING STORIES CALLED PARABLES.

A MAN WAS TRAVELING FROM JERUSALEM DOWN TO JERICHO. THIEVES CAUGHT UP WITH HIM. THEY BEAT HIM, ROBBED HIM, AND LEFT HIM FOR DEAD.

"THE GOOD SAMARITAN"

"A PRIEST HAPPENED TO PASS BY, SAW THE WOUNDED FELLOW, AND WALKED ON BY."

BUT A CERTAIN SAMARITAN, AS HE JOURNEYED, CAME WHERE HE WAS: AND WHEN HE SAW HIM, HE HAD COMPASSION ON HIM.   LUKE 10:33

AND NOT MANY DAYS AFTER THE YOUNGER SON GATHERED ALL TOGETHER, AND TOOK HIS JOURNEY INTO A FAR COUNTRY, AND THERE WASTED HIS SUBSTANCE WITH RIOTOUS LIVING.   LUKE 15:13

FOR THIS MY SON WAS DEAD, AND IS ALIVE AGAIN; HE WAS LOST, AND IS FOUND. AND THEY BEGAN TO BE MERRY.   LUKE 15:24

JESUS AND ZACCHAEUS

AND A CERTAIN RULER ASKED HIM, SAYING, GOOD MASTER, WHAT SHALL I DO TO INHERIT ETERNAL LIFE?   LUKE 18:18

AND, BEHOLD, THERE WAS A MAN NAMED ZACCHAEUS, WHICH WAS THE CHIEF AMONG THE PUBLICANS, AND HE WAS RICH. AND HE SOUGHT TO SEE JESUS WHO HE WAS . . . . LUKE 19:2-3

AND WHEN JESUS CAME TO THE PLACE, HE LOOKED UP, AND SAW HIM, AND SAID UNTO HIM, ZACCHAEUS, MAKE HASTE, AND COME DOWN; FOR TO DAY I MUST ABIDE AT THY HOUSE.   LUKE 19:5

AND ZACCHAEUS STOOD, AND SAID UNTO THE LORD; BEHOLD, LORD, THE HALF OF MY GOODS I GIVE TO THE POOR . . . . LUKE 19:8

Jesus and Zacchaeus Luke 19

JESUS RAISES LAZARUS

THEREFORE HIS SISTERS SENT UNTO HIM, SAYING, LORD, BEHOLD, HE WHOM THOU LOVEST IS SICK.   JOHN 11:3

THREE OF JESUS' FRIENDS ARE LAZARUS, MARY, AND MARTHA. THEY LIVE IN BETHANY, NEAR JERUSALEM.

GO FIND JESUS AND TELL HIM THE ONE HE LOVES IS VERY SICK.

THE SERVANT BRINGS THE NEWS TO JESUS.

LAZARUS WILL NOT DIE. HIS ILLNESS IS FOR GOD'S GLORY.

... HE SAITH UNTO THEM, OUR FRIEND LAZARUS SLEEPETH; BUT I GO, THAT I MAY AWAKE HIM OUT OF SLEEP.   JOHN 11:11

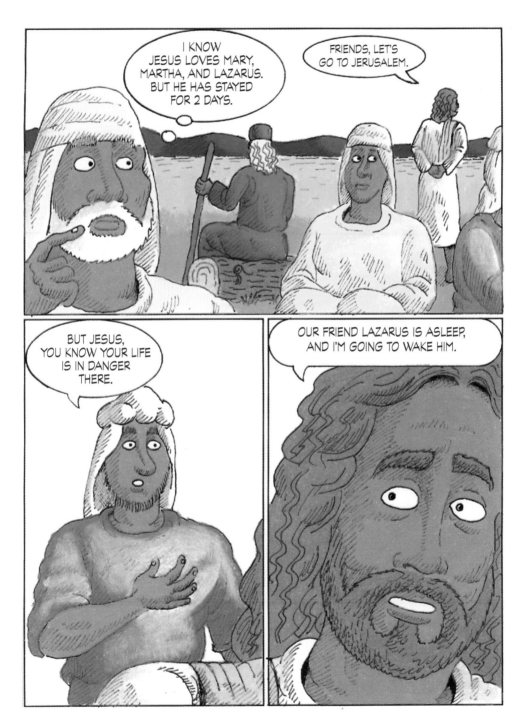

Jesus Raises Lazarus (195) John 11

JESUS SAID UNTO HER, I AM THE RESURRECTION, AND THE LIFE: HE THAT BELIEVETH IN ME, THOUGH HE WERE DEAD, YET SHALL HE LIVE.
JOHN 11:25

AND WHEN HE THUS HAD SPOKEN, HE CRIED WITH A LOUD VOICE, LAZARUS, COME FORTH. AND HE THAT WAS DEAD CAME FORTH, BOUND HAND AND FOOT WITH GRAVECLOTHES . . . .   JOHN 11:43-44

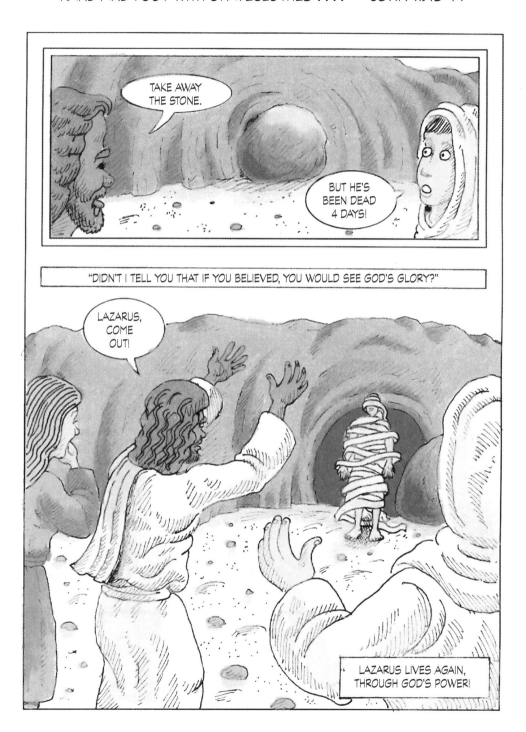

JESUS IN JERUSALEM

... GO YOUR WAY INTO THE VILLAGE OVER AGAINST YOU: AND AS SOON AS YE BE ENTERED INTO IT, YE SHALL FIND A COLT TIED, WHEREON NEVER MAN SAT; LOOSE HIM, AND BRING HIM.   MARK 11:2

AND MANY SPREAD THEIR GARMENTS IN THE WAY: AND OTHERS CUT
DOWN BRANCHES OFF THE TREES, AND STRAWED THEM IN THE WAY.
MARK 11:8

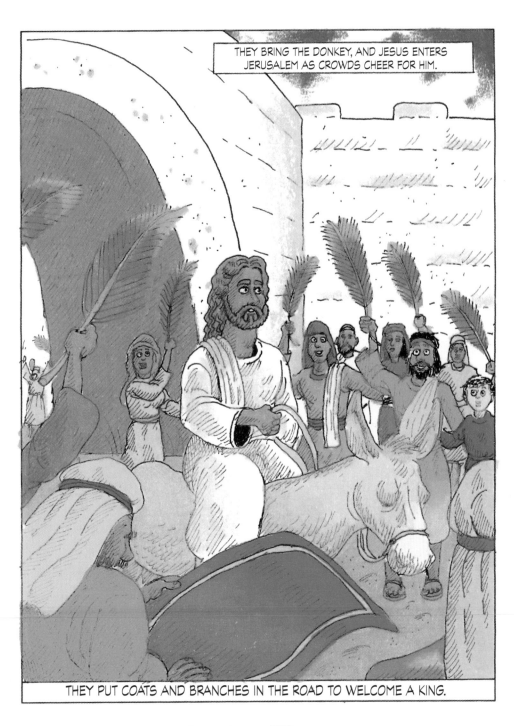

AND HE TAUGHT, SAYING UNTO THEM, IS IT NOT WRITTEN, MY HOUSE
SHALL BE CALLED OF ALL NATIONS THE HOUSE OF PRAYER? BUT YE
HAVE MADE IT A DEN OF THIEVES.   MARK 11:17

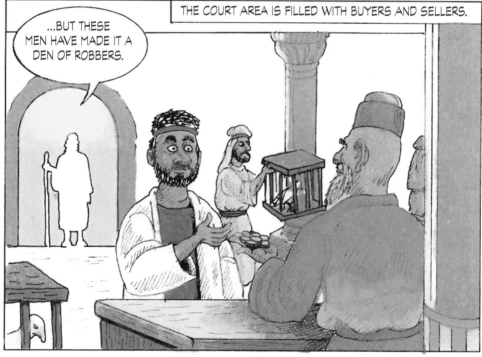

...AND JESUS WENT INTO THE TEMPLE, AND BEGAN TO CAST OUT THEM THAT SOLD AND BOUGHT IN THE TEMPLE, AND OVERTHREW THE TABLES OF THE MONEYCHANGERS.... MARK 11:15

JESUS DRIVES OUT THE MONEY-MAKERS, TOPPLING THEIR TABLES.

DID YOU SEE THE WAY THE PEOPLE LISTEN TO HIM?

WE MUST FIND A WAY TO GET RID OF HIM.

JESUS' LAST SUPPER

NOW THE FIRST DAY OF THE FEAST OF UNLEAVENED BREAD THE DISCIPLES CAME TO JESUS, SAYING UNTO HIM, WHERE WILT THOU THAT WE PREPARE FOR THEE TO EAT THE PASSOVER?   MATTHEW 26:17

NOW WHEN THE EVEN WAS COME, HE SAT DOWN WITH THE TWELVE. AND AS THEY DID EAT, HE SAID, VERILY I SAY UNTO YOU, THAT ONE OF YOU SHALL BETRAY ME.   MATTHEW 26:20-21

JESUS SAID UNTO HIM, VERILY I SAY UNTO THEE, THAT THIS NIGHT, BEFORE THE COCK CROW, THOU SHALT DENY ME THRICE.
MATTHEW 26:34

AND JESUS SAID UNTO HIM, FRIEND, WHEREFORE ART THOU COME? THEN
CAME THEY, AND LAID HANDS ON JESUS, AND TOOK HIM.
MATTHEW 26:50

JESUS IS CRUCIFIED

AND JESUS STOOD BEFORE THE GOVERNOR: AND THE GOVERNOR ASKED HIM, SAYING, ART THOU THE KING OF THE JEWS? AND JESUS SAID UNTO HIM, THOU SAYEST. MATTHEW 27:11

JESUS APPEARS BEFORE THE ELDERS AND HIGH PRIEST.

I COMMAND YOU UNDER OATH TO TELL US: ARE YOU THE SON OF GOD?

IT IS AS YOU SAY. AND IN THE FUTURE YOU WILL SEE THE SON OF MAN COMING ON THE CLOUDS, AND SITTING AT GOD'S RIGHT HAND.

BLASPHEMY!

HE DESERVES DEATH!

HAND HIM OVER TO THE ROMANS!

OUT IN THE COURTYARD, PETER IS NOTICED.

YOU'RE ONE OF JESUS' MEN.

I DON'T KNOW WHAT YOU'RE TALKING ABOUT.

IN FEAR, PETER DENIES HE KNOWS JESUS — JUST AS JESUS PREDICTED.

THEN SAID PILATE UNTO HIM, HEAREST THOU NOT HOW MANY THINGS
THEY WITNESS AGAINST THEE? AND HE ANSWERED HIM TO NEVER A
WORD; INSOMUCH THAT THE GOVERNOR MARVELLED GREATLY.
MATTHEW 27:13-14

JUDAS SEES HOW JESUS IS TREATED AND IS FILLED WITH HORROR.

HE THROWS THE MONEY DOWN, AND TAKES HIS OWN LIFE.

JESUS THEN APPEARS BEFORE PILATE, THE ROMAN GOVERNOR.

ARE YOU THE KING OF THE JEWS?

YES, IT IS AS YOU SAY.

THE CHIEF PRIESTS AND ELDERS YELL INSULTS, BUT JESUS STANDS SILENTLY.

THERE IS AN OLD TRADITION THAT THE GOVERNOR MAY RELEASE ONE PRISONER ON THE PASSOVER FEAST. PILATE WANTS TO AVOID EXECUTING JESUS, SO HE ASKS THE CROWD IF JESUS MIGHT BE RELEASED.

NO! FREE THE OTHER ONE!

BARABBAS!

GIVE US BARABBAS!

DEATH TO JESUS!

BARABBAS, A MURDERER, IS SET FREE INSTEAD.

AND AFTER THAT THEY HAD MOCKED HIM, THEY TOOK THE ROBE OFF FROM HIM, AND PUT HIS OWN RAIMENT ON HIM, AND LED HIM AWAY TO CRUCIFY HIM.   MATTHEW 27:31

THE SOLDIERS MOCK JESUS, PUTTING A RED ROBE AND A PAINFUL CROWN OF THORNS ON HIM. THEY SPIT ON HIM AND BEAT HIM.

HAIL, KING OF THE JEWS!

JESUS IS SENTENCED TO DEATH. HE IS FALSELY ACCUSED OF BEING A TROUBLEMAKER, AND OF SPEAKING BLASPHEMY AGAINST GOD. THE ROMANS EXECUTE CRIMINALS BY NAILING THEM TO WOODEN CROSSES.

THEY FORCE JESUS TO CARRY HIS OWN CROSSBAR.

NOW WHEN THE CENTURION, AND THEY THAT WERE WITH HIM, WATCHING JESUS, SAW THE EARTHQUAKE, AND THOSE THINGS THAT WERE DONE, THEY FEARED GREATLY, SAYING, TRULY THIS WAS THE SON OF GOD.
MATTHEW 27:54

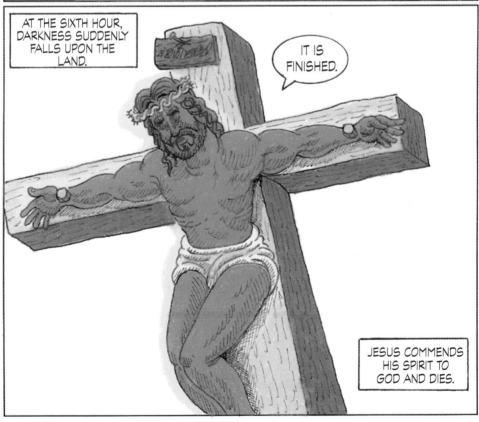

JESUS IS RISEN!

THE FIRST DAY OF THE WEEK COMETH MARY MAGDALENE EARLY, WHEN IT WAS YET DARK, UNTO THE SEPULCHRE, AND SEETH THE STONE TAKEN AWAY FROM THE SEPULCHRE.   JOHN 20:1

NICODEMUS, A PHARISEE WHO HAD VISITED JESUS, AND JOSEPH OF ARIMATHEA ASK FOR JESUS' BODY. THEY WRAP IT BY JEWISH CUSTOM AND BURY HIM.

ON SUNDAY MORNING, MARY MAGDALENE VISITS THE TOMB WHILE IT IS STILL DARK.

BUT... THE STONE IS ROLLED AWAY!

THEN SHE RUNNETH, AND COMETH TO SIMON PETER ... THEY HAVE
TAKEN AWAY THE LORD OUT OF THE SEPULCHRE, AND WE KNOW NOT
WHERE THEY HAVE LAID HIM.   JOHN 20:2

PETER! JOHN!
SOMEONE HAS MOVED
JESUS' BODY, AND I DON'T
KNOW WHERE THEY'VE
TAKEN IT!

JOHN ARRIVES AND SEES THE STRIPS OF
BURIAL LINEN — BUT DOESN'T GO IN.

PETER RUNS INSIDE THE TOMB, THEN JOHN.

ONLY THE BURIAL WRAPPINGS ARE THERE.

AND THEY SAY UNTO HER, WOMAN, WHY WEEPEST THOU? SHE SAITH
UNTO THEM, BECAUSE THEY HAVE TAKEN AWAY MY LORD, AND I KNOW
NOT WHERE THEY HAVE LAID HIM.   JOHN 20:13

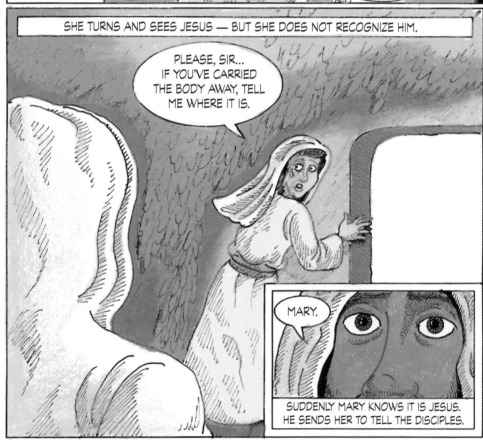

JESUS SAITH UNTO HIM, THOMAS, BECAUSE THOU HAST SEEN ME, THOU HAST BELIEVED: BLESSED ARE THEY THAT HAVE NOT SEEN, AND YET HAVE BELIEVED.   JOHN 20:29

PETER IS FORGIVEN

PETER THEN DENIED AGAIN: AND IMMEDIATELY THE COCK CREW.
JOHN 18:27

PETER IS FILLED WITH MEMORIES OF JESUS.

PETER REMEMBERS STEPPING OUT OF THE BOAT AND — JUST FOR A MOMENT — WALKING WITH JESUS.

... CAST THE NET ON THE RIGHT SIDE OF THE SHIP, AND YE SHALL FIND. THEY CAST THEREFORE, AND NOW THEY WERE NOT ABLE TO DRAW IT FOR THE MULTITUDE OF FISHES.   JOHN 21:6

. . . NOW WHEN SIMON PETER HEARD THAT IT WAS THE LORD, HE GIRT HIS FISHER'S COAT UNTO HIM, (FOR HE WAS NAKED,) AND DID CAST HIMSELF INTO THE SEA.   JOHN 21:7

JOHN IS THE FIRST TO RECOGNIZE THE STRANGER.

IT IS THE LORD!

PETER LEAPS FROM THE BOAT AND SWIMS TO SHORE.

BRING SOME OF YOUR FISH AND WE'LL FIX BREAKFAST.

... JESUS SAITH TO SIMON PETER, SIMON, SON OF JONAS, LOVEST THOU ME MORE THAN THESE? HE SAITH UNTO HIM, YEA, LORD; THOU KNOWEST THAT I LOVE THEE .... JOHN 21:15

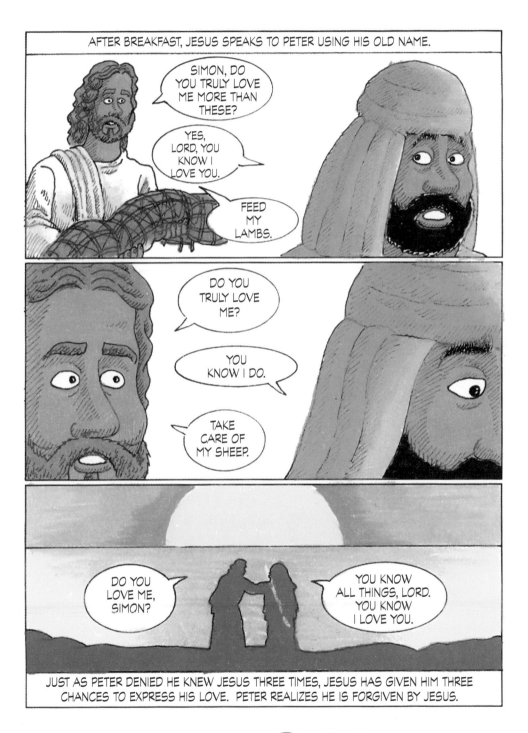

JESUS SENDS THE SPIRIT

AND THAT REPENTANCE AND REMISSION OF SINS SHOULD BE PREACHED
IN HIS NAME AMONG ALL NATIONS, BEGINNING AT JERUSALEM.
LUKE 24:47

TO EVERYONE'S AMAZEMENT, JESUS IS SEEN BY MANY OVER A PERIOD OF
40 DAYS AFTER HIS RESURRECTION.

I SAW HIM DIE ON A CROSS!

YET HE LIVES AGAIN.

HE GIVES HIS FRIENDS INSTRUCTIONS FOR THE FUTURE.

YOU WILL RECEIVE POWER WHEN THE HOLY SPIRIT COMES. AND YOU WILL SPEAK FOR ME...

IN JERUSALEM, THEN IN ALL JUDEA AND SAMARIA, AND THEN TO THE FARTHEST PARTS OF THE WORLD.

... HE LIFTED UP HIS HANDS, AND BLESSED THEM. AND IT CAME TO PASS, WHILE HE BLESSED THEM, HE WAS PARTED FROM THEM, AND CARRIED UP INTO HEAVEN.   LUKE 24:50-51

AFTER JESUS SAYS THIS, HE IS TAKEN UP INTO THE SKY BEFORE THEIR EYES.

SUDDENLY, TWO MEN DRESSED IN WHITE ARE AMONG THEM.

WHY DO YOU LOOK INTO THE SKY?

JESUS WILL RETURN THE SAME WAY HE LEFT.

AND SUDDENLY THERE CAME A SOUND FROM HEAVEN AS OF A RUSHING
MIGHTY WIND, AND IT FILLED ALL THE HOUSE WHERE THEY
WERE SITTING.   ACTS 2:2

. . . REPENT, AND BE BAPTIZED EVERY ONE OF YOU IN THE NAME OF JESUS CHRIST FOR THE REMISSION OF SINS, AND YE SHALL RECEIVE THE GIFT OF THE HOLY GHOST.   ACTS 2:38

THE FIRST CHRISTIANS

AND STEPHEN, FULL OF FAITH AND POWER, DID GREAT WONDERS AND MIRACLES AMONG THE PEOPLE.   ACTS 6:8

THE TEACHINGS OF CHRIST ARE SWEEPING JERUSALEM. AS THE YOUNG CHURCH GROWS, THE DISCIPLES APPOINT 7 MEN TO SERVE AS DEACONS.

ONE OF THOSE DEACONS, STEPHEN, IS A MAN OF STRONG FAITH. THE ENEMIES OF THE CHURCH TAKE NOTICE OF HIM.

AND THEY STIRRED UP THE PEOPLE, AND THE ELDERS, AND THE SCRIBES,
AND CAME UPON HIM, AND CAUGHT HIM, AND BROUGHT HIM
TO THE COUNCIL.   ACTS 6:12

AND HE KNEELED DOWN, AND CRIED WITH A LOUD VOICE, LORD, LAY
NOT THIS SIN TO THEIR CHARGE. AND WHEN HE HAD SAID THIS,
HE FELL ASLEEP.   ACTS 7:60

AS FOR SAUL, HE MADE HAVOCK OF THE CHURCH, ENTERING INTO EVERY HOUSE, AND HALING MEN AND WOMEN COMMITTED THEM TO PRISON.
ACTS 8:3

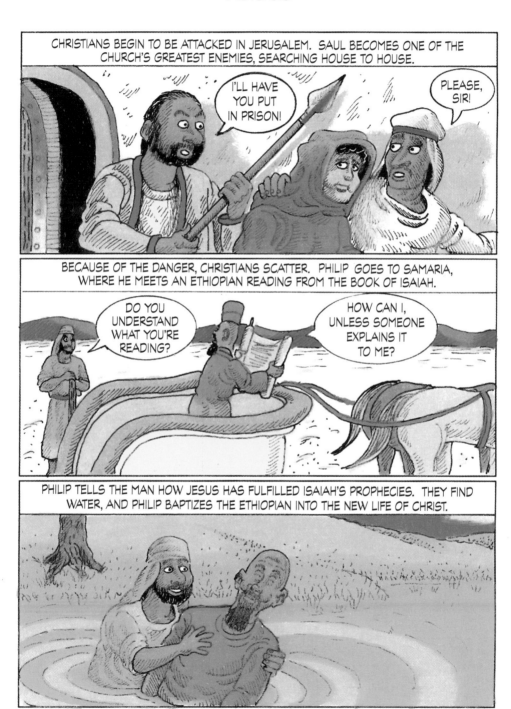

PAUL MEETS CHRIST

AND SAUL, YET BREATHING OUT THREATENINGS AND SLAUGHTER AGAINST THE DISCIPLES OF THE LORD, WENT UNTO THE HIGH PRIEST, AND DESIRED OF HIM LETTERS TO DAMASCUS TO THE SYNAGOGUES . . . .

ACTS 9:1-2

SAUL HAS DEVOTED HIS LIFE TO HURTING CHRISTIANS.

I WISH TO TRAVEL TO DAMASCUS AND FIND CHRISTIANS THERE. I'LL BRING THEM BACK TO JERUSALEM AS PRISONERS.

SAUL, YOU ARE A DEDICATED SERVANT OF GOD.

IT IS A LONG JOURNEY NORTHWARD TO DAMASCUS.

. . . AND SUDDENLY THERE SHINED ROUND ABOUT HIM A LIGHT FROM HEAVEN: AND HE FELL TO THE EARTH, AND HEARD A VOICE SAYING UNTO HIM, SAUL, SAUL, WHY PERSECUTEST THOU ME?   **ACTS 9:3-4**

AND SAUL AROSE FROM THE EARTH; AND WHEN HIS EYES WERE OPENED, HE SAW NO MAN: BUT THEY LED HIM BY THE HAND, AND BROUGHT HIM INTO DAMASCUS.   ACTS 9:8

AND IMMEDIATELY THERE FELL FROM HIS EYES AS IT HAD BEEN SCALES: AND HE RECEIVED SIGHT FORTHWITH, AND AROSE, AND WAS BAPTIZED. ACTS 9:18

PETER HAS A VISION

AND WHEN SAUL WAS COME TO JERUSALEM, HE ASSAYED TO JOIN HIMSELF TO THE DISCIPLES: BUT THEY WERE ALL AFRAID OF HIM, AND BELIEVED NOT THAT HE WAS A DISCIPLE.   ACTS 9:26

PAUL, THE NEW CHRISTIAN, TRAVELS TO JERUSALEM. THE DISCIPLES FEAR HIM.

LET ME IN! I KNOW CHRIST NOW, TOO!

CAN OUR ENEMY HAVE CHANGED SO MUCH?

PAUL IS ACCEPTED, AND THEY TALK OF THEIR PLANS FOR THE CHURCH.

WE MUST TELL ALL THE WORLD ABOUT JESUS — NOT JUST THE JEWS!

BUT — ALL THE DISCIPLES ARE JEWS!

AND SAW HEAVEN OPENED, AND A CERTAIN VESSEL DESCENDING UNTO
HIM, AS IT HAD BEEN A GREAT SHEET KNIT AT THE FOUR CORNERS,
AND LET DOWN TO THE EARTH.   ACTS 10:11

CORNELIUS, A GODLY CENTURION, HAS A VISION.

CORNELIUS, YOUR OFFERINGS TO THE POOR HAVE PLEASED GOD. NOW, SEND FOR A MAN NAMED SIMON PETER.

AS THREE MEN TRAVEL TO FIND PETER, PETER ALSO HAS A VISION.

A SHEET COMING DOWN FROM HEAVEN...HOLDING ALL KINDS OF FOOD.

KILL AND EAT, PETER!

MANY OF THE FOODS ON THE SHEET, PETER KNOWS, WOULD BE CONSIDERED
IMPURE AND UNFIT ACCORDING TO HEBREW LAW.

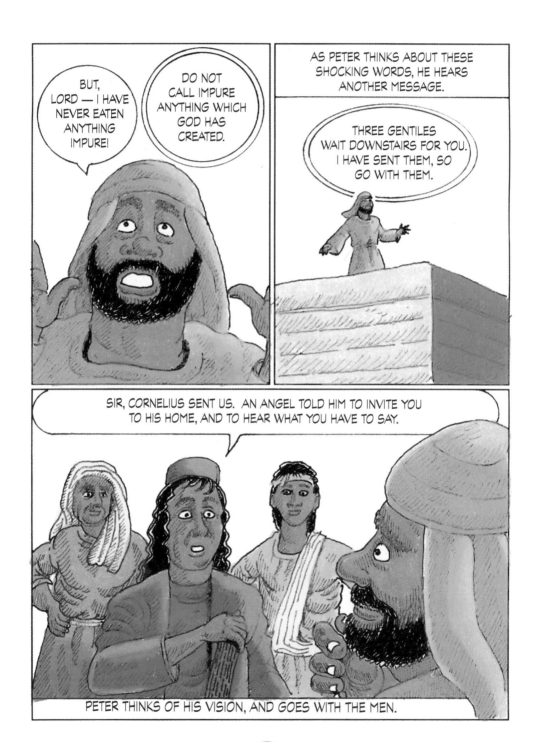

Peter Has a Vision   232   Acts 10

... OF A TRUTH I PERCEIVE THAT GOD IS NO RESPECTER OF PERSONS: BUT IN EVERY NATION HE THAT FEARETH HIM, AND WORKETH RIGHTEOUSNESS, IS ACCEPTED WITH HIM.   ACTS 10:34-35

Peter Has a Vision   (233)   Acts 10

PETER AND THE ANGEL

PETER THEREFORE WAS KEPT IN PRISON: BUT PRAYER WAS
MADE WITHOUT CEASING OF THE CHURCH UNTO GOD FOR HIM.
ACTS 12:5

AND, BEHOLD, THE ANGEL OF THE LORD CAME UPON HIM, AND A LIGHT
SHINED IN THE PRISON: AND HE SMOTE PETER ON THE SIDE,
AND RAISED HIM UP.   ACTS 12:7

Peter and the Angel (235) Acts 12

WHEN THEY WERE PAST THE FIRST AND THE SECOND WARD, THEY CAME UNTO
THE IRON GATE THAT LEADETH UNTO THE CITY; WHICH OPENED TO THEM
OF HIS OWN ACCORD . . . .   ACTS 12:10

BUT PETER CONTINUED KNOCKING: AND WHEN THEY HAD OPENED THE DOOR, AND SAW HIM, THEY WERE ASTONISHED.   ACTS 12:16

Peter and the Angel   237   Acts 12

PAUL'S FIRST JOURNEY

AS THEY MINISTERED TO THE LORD, AND FASTED, THE HOLY GHOST SAID,
SEPARATE ME BARNABAS AND SAUL FOR THE WORK WHEREUNTO I HAVE
CALLED THEM.   ACTS 13:2

THE HOLY SPIRIT SAYS TO THE CHRISTIANS AT ANTIOCH: "SET APART BARNABAS
AND PAUL FOR THE WORK TO WHICH I HAVE CALLED THEM." THE CHURCH FASTS,
PRAYS, THEN LAYS HANDS ON THESE TWO.

THE CHURCH IS SENDING OUT THE FIRST MISSIONARIES.

FOR SO HATH THE LORD COMMANDED US, SAYING, I HAVE SET THEE TO BE A LIGHT OF THE GENTILES, THAT THOU SHOULDEST BE FOR SALVATION UNTO THE ENDS OF THE EARTH.   ACTS 13:47

AND WHEN THE GENTILES HEARD THIS, THEY WERE GLAD, AND
GLORIFIED THE WORD OF THE LORD: AND AS MANY AS WERE
ORDAINED TO ETERNAL LIFE BELIEVED.   ACTS 13:48

THE GENTILES ACCEPT PAUL'S PREACHING GLADLY, AND BEGIN STARTING CHURCHES.
BUT JEWISH LEADERS MAKE TROUBLE, AND THE TWO GO TO THE NEXT CITY.

THROUGHOUT THEIR TRAVELS, PAUL AND HIS FRIENDS PREACH AND HEAL. THEY
FACE MANY DANGERS, BUT CONTINUE TO BOLDLY SPREAD THE GOSPEL.

BLACK SEA

THE
GREAT
SEA

CHURCHES ARE BORN ALL
OVER THE KNOWN WORLD.

JERUSALEM

PAUL'S SHIPWRECK

AND WHEN IT WAS DETERMINED THAT WE SHOULD SAIL INTO ITALY, THEY
DELIVERED PAUL AND CERTAIN OTHER PRISONERS UNTO ONE NAMED
JULIUS, A CENTURION OF AUGUSTUS' BAND.   ACTS 27:1

AND NOW I EXHORT YOU TO BE OF GOOD CHEER: FOR THERE SHALL BE
NO LOSS OF ANY MAN'S LIFE AMONG YOU, BUT OF THE SHIP.
ACTS 27:22

PAUL WARNS THE CREW.

WE'RE GETTING A LATE START. WE COULD FACE WINTER STORMS AND BE KILLED!

SORRY, I HAVE ORDERS.

THE STORM COMES, AND IT'S A BAD ONE. AFTER MANY DAYS, THE MEN BEGIN TO LOSE HOPE. BUT PAUL IS AN ENCOURAGER.

BE BRAVE, MEN. GOD WILL PROTECT US, AND I WILL STAND BEFORE CAESAR IN ROME. AN ANGEL TOLD ME THIS.

Paul's Shipwreck (243) Acts 27

AND THE REST, SOME ON BOARDS, AND SOME ON BROKEN PIECES OF
THE SHIP. AND SO IT CAME TO PASS, THAT THEY ESCAPED ALL SAFE
TO LAND.   ACTS 27:44

AND PAUL DWELT TWO WHOLE YEARS IN HIS OWN HIRED HOUSE
... PREACHING THE KINGDOM OF GOD, AND TEACHING THOSE THINGS
WHICH CONCERN THE LORD JESUS CHRIST ....   ACTS 28:30-31

PAUL BUILDS A FIRE FOR WARMTH. THE HEAT ATTRACTS A SNAKE, WHICH BITES PAUL'S HAND. THE OTHERS SEE IT AS A SIGN FROM GOD.

LOOK! GOD MUST WANT THE PRISONER KILLED AFTER ALL!

BUT THE BITE HAS NO EFFECT ON PAUL — SO NOW THE MEN THINK HE IS A GOD. PAUL AND THE OTHERS ARE TAKEN TO A HOME NEARBY WHERE PAUL HEALS THE OWNER'S SICK FATHER.

THIS PAUL CAN DO ANYTHING!

AFTER WINTER, THE CREW AND PRISONERS SAIL AGAIN IN A NEW SHIP. PAUL IS A PRISONER IN ROME — YET HE CONTINUES TO PREACH THE GOSPEL AND CHANGE THE WORLD.

Paul's Shipwreck   245   Acts 27

THE MINISTRY OF PAUL

AND THERE CAME THITHER CERTAIN JEWS FROM ANTIOCH AND ICONIUM, WHO PERSUADED THE PEOPLE, AND, HAVING STONED PAUL, DREW HIM OUT OF THE CITY.   **ACTS 14:19**

THE BOOK OF ACTS TELLS OF PAUL'S MISSIONARY JOURNEYS. HE HAS MANY ADVENTURES. CLEVERLY, HE SPEAKS TO PEOPLE USING THEIR OWN IDEAS.

YOU GREEKS HAVE STATUES FOR ALL THE GODS — EVEN AN "UNKNOWN GOD!" I'M HERE TO TELL YOU WHO THAT UNKNOWN GOD IS...

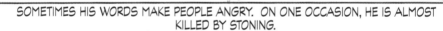

SOMETIMES HIS WORDS MAKE PEOPLE ANGRY. ON ONE OCCASION, HE IS ALMOST KILLED BY STONING.

THEN THE DISCIPLES TOOK HIM BY NIGHT, AND LET HIM DOWN BY THE
WALL IN A BASKET.   ACTS 9:25

ANOTHER TIME, PAUL FINDS OUT ABOUT A PLOT TO KILL HIM. FRIENDS HELP HIM
ESCAPE IN A BASKET, LOWERED THROUGH A HOLE IN THE CITY WALL.

HE IS OFTEN ACCUSED AND BROUGHT TO TRIAL BEFORE THE ROMANS.
HE TAKES THESE OPPORTUNITIES TO TALK ABOUT JESUS.

THAT IF THOU SHALT CONFESS WITH THY MOUTH THE LORD JESUS, AND SHALT BELIEVE IN THINE HEART THAT GOD HATH RAISED HIM FROM THE DEAD, THOU SHALT BE SAVED.   ROMANS 10:9

AND HAVING THIS CONFIDENCE, I KNOW THAT I SHALL ABIDE AND
CONTINUE WITH YOU ALL FOR YOUR FURTHERANCE AND JOY OF FAITH.
PHILIPPIANS 1:25

THE OTHER CHURCHES SHARE PAUL'S LETTERS, COPYING THEM AND PASSING THEM ON.

PHILIPPIANS SPEAKS OF JOY IN CHRIST — A JOY WE CAN HAVE NO MATTER WHAT HAPPENS IN LIFE.

HE TELLS THE THESSALONIANS TO STAND FIRM IN TOUGH TIMES. AFTER ALL, WE NEVER KNOW WHEN THE LORD WILL RETURN!

PAUL DIRECTS HIS YOUNG FRIENDS TIMOTHY AND TITUS ON WHAT KINDS OF LEADERS THE CHURCH SHOULD HAVE. PHILEMON TELLS OF FORGIVENESS.

PAUL'S WORDS HELP US BUILD STRONG CHURCHES AND CHRISTIANS.

LETTERS FOR LIVING

SIMON PETER, A SERVANT AND AN APOSTLE OF JESUS CHRIST, TO THEM THAT HAVE OBTAINED LIKE PRECIOUS FAITH WITH US THROUGH THE RIGHTEOUSNESS OF GOD AND OUR SAVIOUR JESUS CHRIST.

2 PETER 1:1

DURING THE FIRST CENTURY, THE YOUNG CHURCHES SEEK TO APPLY JESUS' TEACHINGS TO LIFE. PAUL AND THE OTHER APOSTLES OFFER GUIDANCE AND ENCOURAGEMENT IN LETTERS SHARED AMONG THE CHURCHES.

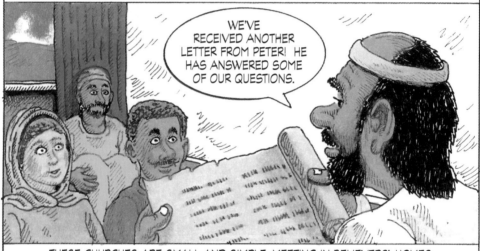

WE'VE RECEIVED ANOTHER LETTER FROM PETER! HE HAS ANSWERED SOME OF OUR QUESTIONS.

THESE CHURCHES ARE SMALL AND SIMPLE, MEETING IN BELIEVERS' HOMES.

THE LETTER TO THE <u>HEBREWS</u> HAS THIS MESSAGE: LIFE IS DIFFICULT, BUT KEEP THE FAITH! REMEMBER THE FAITH HEROES OF THE PAST — ABRAHAM, MOSES, AND ALL THE OTHERS.

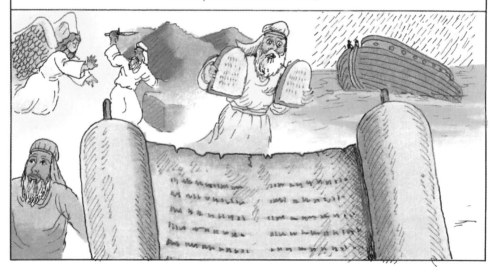

BUT BE YE DOERS OF THE WORD, AND NOT HEARERS ONLY, DECEIVING
YOUR OWN SELVES.   JAMES 1:22

THE LETTER FROM <u>JAMES</u>, THE BROTHER OF JESUS, REMINDS US TO
BE A DOER OF GOD'S WORD, NOT JUST A HEARER. FAITH WITHOUT
ACTION IS WORTHLESS. WE SHOW OUR FAITH IN CARING FOR WIDOWS
AND ORPHANS, AND CONTROLLING OUR SPEECH.

<u>PETER</u>, THE APOSTLE, IS THE AUTHOR OF TWO LETTERS. PETER ENCOURAGES
PERSECUTED BELIEVERS TO BE HOLY. IT IS AN HONOR TO SUFFER FOR CHRIST.

BUT IF WE WALK IN THE LIGHT, AS HE IS IN THE LIGHT, WE HAVE FELLOWSHIP ONE WITH ANOTHER, AND THE BLOOD OF JESUS CHRIST HIS SON CLEANSETH US FROM ALL SIN.   1 JOHN 1:7

JUDE WRITES THAT WE SHOULD BE SERIOUS ABOUT CHRISTIAN TEACHING, AVOIDING THE IDEAS OF GODLESS PEOPLE.

JOHN, THE BELOVED DISCIPLE, IS THE AUTHOR OF A GOSPEL, THREE LETTERS, AND REVELATION. HIS BEAUTIFUL LETTERS TEACH US TO WALK IN THE LIGHT, AND TO LOVE ONE ANOTHER. WE ARE THE CHILDREN OF GOD.

AND GOD SHALL WIPE AWAY ALL TEARS FROM THEIR EYES; AND THERE SHALL BE NO MORE DEATH, NEITHER SORROW, NOR CRYING, NEITHER SHALL THERE BE ANY MORE PAIN . . . .   REVELATION 21:4

THE LAST LIVING DISCIPLE, JOHN, RECEIVES A <u>REVELATION</u> FROM GOD — A GLIMPSE INTO THE FUTURE. STAND FIRM IN PERSECUTION, JOHN TELLS THE CHURCHES. CHRIST WILL RETURN IN VICTORY!

"THEN I SAW A NEW HEAVEN AND A NEW EARTH. HE SAID, 'I AM MAKING EVERYTHING NEW.'"

"HE WILL WIPE AWAY EVERY TEAR — NO MORE DEATH, OR CRYING, OR PAIN. THE OLD HAS PASSED AWAY."

"YES, I AM COMING SOON. THE GRACE OF THE LORD JESUS BE WITH GOD'S PEOPLE, AMEN."

Rob Suggs 8-15-95

THE WORLD OF GENESIS

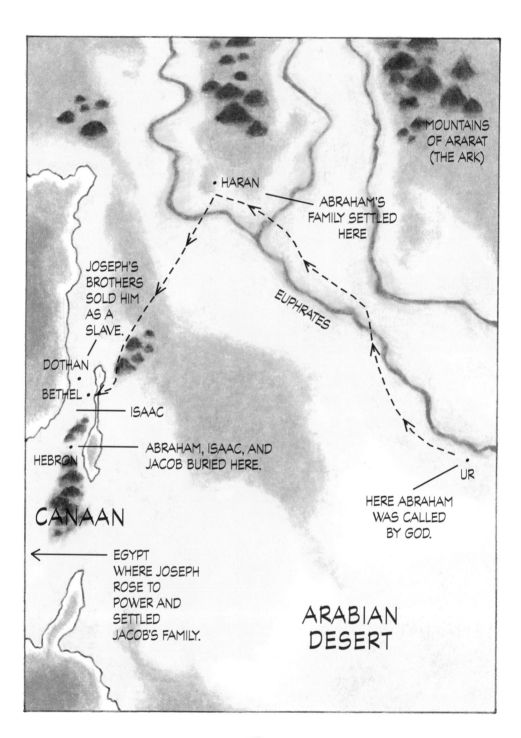

MOUNTAINS OF ARARAT (THE ARK)

HARAN

ABRAHAM'S FAMILY SETTLED HERE

JOSEPH'S BROTHERS SOLD HIM AS A SLAVE.

EUPHRATES

DOTHAN

BETHEL ISAAC

HEBRON ABRAHAM, ISAAC, AND JACOB BURIED HERE.

UR

HERE ABRAHAM WAS CALLED BY GOD.

CANAAN

EGYPT WHERE JOSEPH ROSE TO POWER AND SETTLED JACOB'S FAMILY.

ARABIAN DESERT

TEN COMMANDMENTS

I AM
THE LORD YOUR GOD:

YOU WILL HONOR
NO OTHER GODS.

YOU WILL MAKE
NO IDOLS.

YOU WILL NOT
MISUSE MY NAME.

YOU WILL KEEP
THE SABBATH
HOLY.

YOU WILL HONOR
YOUR PARENTS.

YOU WILL NOT
KILL.

YOU WILL NOT
COMMIT ADULTERY.

YOU WILL NOT
STEAL.

YOU WILL NOT LIE.

YOU WILL NOT
LONG FOR YOUR
NEIGHBORS
THINGS.

FAMILY LIFE IN ISRAEL

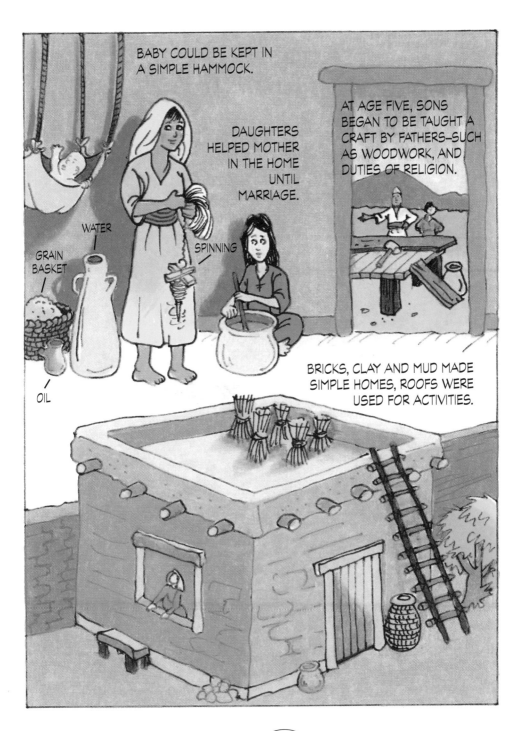

BABY COULD BE KEPT IN A SIMPLE HAMMOCK.

DAUGHTERS HELPED MOTHER IN THE HOME UNTIL MARRIAGE.

AT AGE FIVE, SONS BEGAN TO BE TAUGHT A CRAFT BY FATHERS—SUCH AS WOODWORK, AND DUTIES OF RELIGION.

WATER

SPINNING

GRAIN BASKET

OIL

BRICKS, CLAY AND MUD MADE SIMPLE HOMES, ROOFS WERE USED FOR ACTIVITIES.

THE 23ᴿᴰ PSALM

The Lord is my shepherd;
I shall not want. He maketh me to
lie down in green pastures:
he leadeth me beside the still waters.
He restoreth my soul: he leadeth me in the
paths of righteousness for his name's sake.
Yea, though I walk through the valley of the
shadow of death, I will fear no evil:
for thou art with me; thy rod and thy staff
they comfort me. Thou preparest a table
before me in the presence of mine enemies:
thou anointest my head with oil; my cup
runneth over. Surely goodness and mercy
shall follow me all the days
of my life: and I will dwell
in the house of the Lord
for ever.

SHEPHERDS AND FISHERMEN

STAFF FOR CLIMBING, HERDING.

WATER.

LEATHER BAG.

DAVID AND MOSES WERE TWO OF THE BIBLE'S SHEPHERDS. KEEPING SHEEP TOOK TRAINING AND DEDICATION. A SHEPHERD KNEW EACH OF HIS SHEEP WELL. AND THEY KNEW AND ANSWERED ONLY HIS VOICE, HE WOULD RISK HIS LIFE TO RESCUE A SHEEP FROM A CLIFF OR WILD ANIMAL. JESUS IS OUR "GOOD SHEPHERD."

JESUS SAID; "I WILL MAKE YOU FISHERS OF MEN." MATTHEW 4:19

FISHERMEN CAST THEIR NETS IN HOPE OF A BOUNTY OF FISH FOR THE MARKET. FISHING WAS OFTEN DONE AT NIGHT WITH TORCHLIGHT. IT WAS HARD LABOR.

SOLDIERS IN BIBLE TIMES

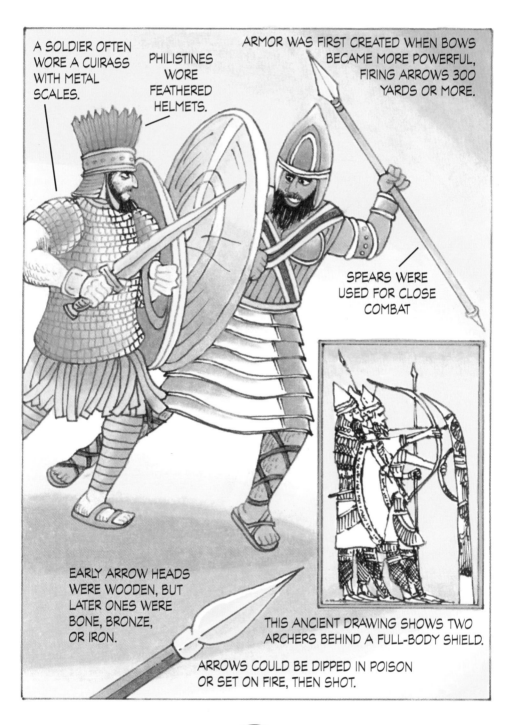

A SOLDIER OFTEN WORE A CUIRASS WITH METAL SCALES.

PHILISTINES WORE FEATHERED HELMETS.

ARMOR WAS FIRST CREATED WHEN BOWS BECAME MORE POWERFUL, FIRING ARROWS 300 YARDS OR MORE.

SPEARS WERE USED FOR CLOSE COMBAT

EARLY ARROW HEADS WERE WOODEN, BUT LATER ONES WERE BONE, BRONZE, OR IRON.

THIS ANCIENT DRAWING SHOWS TWO ARCHERS BEHIND A FULL-BODY SHIELD.

ARROWS COULD BE DIPPED IN POISON OR SET ON FIRE, THEN SHOT.

THE LIFE OF JESUS

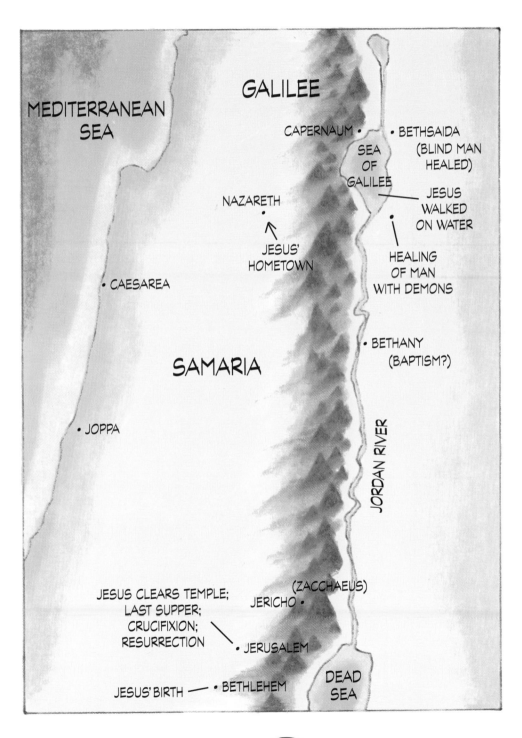

MEDITERRANEAN
SEA

GALILEE

CAPERNAUM •   • BETHSAIDA
(BLIND MAN
HEALED)

SEA
OF
GALILEE

JESUS
WALKED
ON WATER

NAZARETH
•

↑
JESUS'
HOMETOWN

HEALING
OF MAN
WITH DEMONS

• CAESAREA

SAMARIA

• BETHANY
(BAPTISM?)

• JOPPA

JORDAN RIVER

JESUS CLEARS TEMPLE;
LAST SUPPER;
CRUCIFIXION;
RESURRECTION

(ZACCHAEUS)

JERICHO •

• JERUSALEM

JESUS' BIRTH — • BETHLEHEM

DEAD
SEA

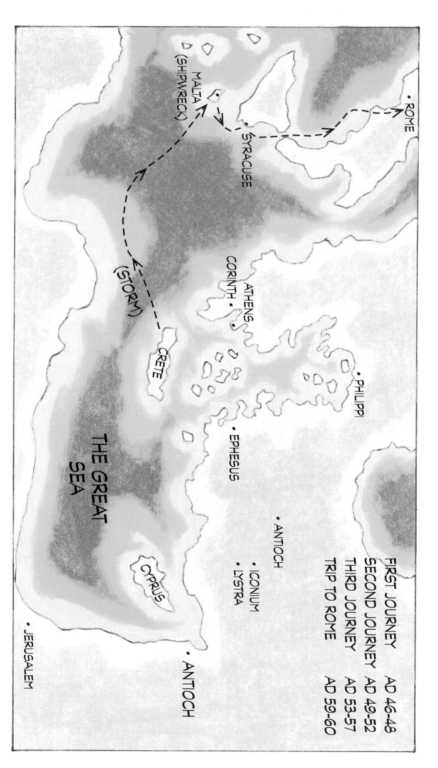

PAUL'S MISSIONARY JOURNEYS

FIRST JOURNEY — AD 46-48
SECOND JOURNEY — AD 49-52
THIRD JOURNEY — AD 53-57
TRIP TO ROME — AD 59-60

ROME

SYRACUSE

MALTA
(SHIPWRECK)

(STORM)

CRETE

ATHENS
CORINTH

PHILIPPI

EPHESUS

THE GREAT
SEA

ANTIOCH
ICONIUM
LYSTRA

CYPRUS

JERUSALEM

ANTIOCH

For God so loved the world, that he gave his only begotten Son, that whosoever believeth in him should not perish, but have everlasting life. John 3:16

Love one another. 1 John 4:7

All scripture is given by inspiration of God, and is profitable for doctrine, for reproof, for correction, for instruction in righteousness. 2 Timothy 3:16

Children, obey your parents in the Lord, for this is right. Ephesians 6:1

Thou shalt love the Lord thy God with all thy heart, and with all thy soul, and with all thy strength, and with all thy mind; and thy neighbour as thyself. Luke 10:27

Trust in the LORD with all thine heart; and lean not unto thine own understanding. In all thy ways acknowledge him, and he shall direct thy paths. Proverbs 3: 5,6

The grass withereth, and the flower fadeth: but the word of our God shall stand for ever. Isaiah 40:8

Rob Suggs keeps busy as a full-time freelance author and illustrator. His entertaining titles include *It Came from Beneath the Pew, Preacher from the Black Lagoon, Murphy Goes to Church,* and *The Adventures of Brother Biddle.* Rob shares his home in Atlanta, Georgia, with his wife, two children, and a 200 pound cat.

Christopher Gray is an illustrator and writer and owner of Scribble Boy Studios, a company dedicated to producing quality books for children. For the past eleven years he has worked in television, magazine, and corporate advertising, creating identities for several major corporations. Christopher, his wife, Kristine, and their two children, live in Carol Stream, Illinois.